PAINTING FURNITURE

PAINTING FURNITURE
A Practical Guide
With Hundreds of Ideas for Creating and Decorating
with Faux Finishes and Painted Effects

Rosie Fisher

LITTLE, BROWN AND COMPANY
Boston New York Toronto London

To Anthony Fisher – a great Grandfather, a great
Father and a great Father-in-Law . . . with Love.

FIRST PAPERBACK EDITION
ISBN 0 316 28378 9 hc
ISBN 0 316 28388 6 pbk

Library of Congress Catalog Number
88–51158

PRINTED IN ITALY

CONTENTS

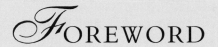OREWORD

Paint glorious paint! There is nothing quite like it for instant results – it's a great master of camouflage. To glance through a paint chart with its choice of delicious colours is, for me, far more exciting than a jeweller's window!

I have always loved colour, and I feel sure it is because, having been born in Egypt, as a child I was dragged round many a painted and decorated tomb, temple and museum. The ultimate treat was a trip to the famous Groppi's sweet shop in Cairo, whose exterior was beautifully hand-painted in brightly coloured flowers. On returning many years later I realised what a profound effect this early 'brainwashing' had had on me.

Today, painted furniture is enjoying a great revival, with many trying their hand and more and more courses on offer. This pleasurable hobby has the added advantage that you will give dull, perhaps discarded pieces of furniture a new lease of life. And you should feel a great sense of achievement. Start with a small piece of furniture, such as a box or mirror, so that you don't find the task too daunting. Don't be over-ambitious or you might put yourself off forever! With something small you will get results fairly quickly, and hopefully be inspired to go on to bigger and better things.

At my shop, Dragons of Walton Street, Chelsea, where we specialise in painted furniture, we started with small painted and decorated chairs for children. Now, ten years later, we can paint any design and finish required. Often, artist and client combined come up with truly imaginative ideas which we are really enthusiastic about trying. Painting furniture is never boring as there are always different finishes to try, fabulous colours to choose from and such a variety of designs to work with. Painting never need become repetitive.

Be a little careful what you paint. Perhaps you don't much like the chair your great-aunt gave you because the paint has worn off, but it may be a valuable Chippendale or Sheraton piece that you would de-value enormously should you smother it in twentieth-century paint! If in doubt, consult an antique dealer. Antique markets and second-hand shops are a good source for the odd paintable piece. Once you are well practised, do invest in the very best you can afford as it is such a waste of time and effort painting a piece if it collapses in a few years. So often artists bring me items to look at and though the artwork is brilliant the piece of furniture should have been burnt long ago!

I do hope you will find that Painting Furniture *arouses and motivates you to pick up a paint brush and express your (perhaps!) hidden talents…Have fun!*

Rosie Fisher, Walton Street, London, Autumn 1988.

Introduction

The ancient Egyptians were the first civilisation to paint furniture, some 3,000 years ago, when they perfected what we now know as 'broken colour techniques' on coffers, chairs, coffins and many smaller objects. To achieve a high quality finish, they coated the article to be painted with a thin layer of adhesive plaster, which provided a very smooth surface on which to apply pigment and helped to produce a beautiful sheen when dry. Using this technique, they were able to imitate the swirling flow of marble and the grain of many woods (real wood was hard to come by in ancient Egypt), in addition to painting more formal motifs and designs on their furniture.

About 2,000 years ago the Chinese developed a new method of painting furniture – the art of lacquering. To the sap of the sumac plant (*Rhus vernicifera*) they added either cinnabar or charred bone meal, to produce a red or black coloured liquid called lacquer. Then they applied a coat of this to the smooth, highly polished wooden surface of a piece of furniture, and left it to dry. When dry, they buffed the surface and applied another coat – repeating the process as many as fifteen times before decorating the piece with motifs and patterns. After decoration, they added up to a further five coats of lacquer, to produce a deep and lustrous finish.

THE INFLUENCE OF CHINESE ART ON THE WEST

Although Europeans became interested in the decorative techniques of the ancient Egyptians, it was artefacts from the Far East that provided the greatest source of fascination and the strongest influence on interior decoration. In the sixteenth century, the first *objets de Chine* (delicate porcelain objects) were introduced to the courts of Europe by the English, Dutch and French East India companies. These same trading companies also imported lacquered furniture, often featuring flower and fruit motifs.

A passion for all things oriental grew during the seventeenth century, especially at the court of Louis XIV, and soon many other European courts boasted a Chinese-style room or pavilion – the first being built for Madame de Pompadour at the palace of Versailles.

Vernis Martin

Supplies of lacquered furniture from the Orient could not keep up with demand, and European furniture makers began to develop their own methods of lacquering. The most successful of these was *vernis Martin*, a technique perfected by the French Martin brothers at the beginning of the eighteenth century. It involved mixing a colour – often green – with varnish and applying the liquid to the buffed, varnished surface of a piece of furniture. Usually, gold dust was added to the undercoats to obtain a more oriental look, and the base of the piece was decorated with arabesque designs, and elaborate pastoral and naturalistic motifs.

Commodes, chairs, tables, many smaller objects, and even carriages were decorated in *vernis Martin*, whether by the brothers or other cabinet makers who copied them. The look became part of the curvaceous excesses of the playful Rococo style, with its carved and painted shells, waves and rocks.

Left: This Louis XV writing desk was given a black lacquer base and then gilded with ornate motifs. Opposite right: A Louis XVI armoire lacquered in vernis Martin, *by F. Duhamel, circa 1750. The characteristic green-coloured ground was gilded with floral and musical motifs down the sides and along the base.*

Above: This eighteenth-century writing box was lacquered in the Venetian lacca povera *style, and then little scenes were painted onto each drawer.*

Above: The influence of Chinese art can be seen in this faux *bamboo chair – to be found in the Brighton Pavilion, England.*

Simulated tortoiseshell

Some of the oriental furniture that found its way into the European courts featured panels, mounted in ivory or ebony, painted in imitation of tortoiseshell. Small pieces and boxes were decorated entirely in this exquisite style, which became immensely popular because of its opulent appearance. European craftmen soon discovered that in order to achieve the most effective results the technique had to be applied with restraint; that is, confined to fairly small objects or areas. However, their lacquered tortoiseshell boxes rarely achieved the high quality of the oriental originals.

Japanning

In Britain, cabinet makers developed their own method of imitating oriental lacquer, known as japanning, by using a combination of varnish (obtained from the resin deposited on trees by the insect *Coccus lacca*) and various pigments available from Europe.

Japanned furniture became popular during the reign of William and Mary (1689–1702), when many cabinet makers followed the instructions given by John Stalker and George Parker in their work '*Treatise on Japanning and Varnishing*'.

The authors advised that the surface of any piece to be japanned must be highly polished and varnished; gave the sources of pigments for background colours – the most common of which were black, red, green and white – and advised on the best colours to use for any painted motifs, depending on the background colour. They also recommended thickening the metallic powder used for the motif(s) with gum Arabic – instructing the artisan to apply this mixture to the japanned surface and then to draw his design in it with a stylus, so that it stood out in relief. When dry, they advised he should polish and gild the piece to finish it off.

The Depentori

The first craftsmen in Italy to imitate oriental lacquering were the Venetian *depentori*, who began to offer their services at the beginning of the eighteenth century. Their technique consisted of coating the already-sanded wood of the piece to be painted with gesso (a mixture of glue and plaster-of-Paris), and letting it dry. After further sanding, sheets of linen were glued to the surface and the background colour laid down – often in cream, pale green, yellow, ivory, pale blue or pink. On top of this the motifs were painted in tempera – the fanciful designs being filled in with a vivid colour, and outlined in a darker shade using a goose feather. Finally, the piece was varnished with sandarac (a conifer resin).

By the middle of the eighteenth century, lacquered furniture and household objects were so much in demand that the Venetian craftsmen had to look for ways of speeding up the process, and thus *lacca contrafatta* was born. Instead of coloured motifs being painted on top of the background colour, they were cut out and glued in position. After many coats of varnish, the cut-outs resembled hand-painted decoration.

Faux bamboo

Bamboo furniture also found its way into Europe via the East India companies, and was much in demand by the middle of the seventeenth century. Again, demand exceeded supply and craftsmen began to imitate bamboo, using turned wood and plaster-of-Paris for the joints.

However, *faux* bamboo did not really come into its own in England until the Regency period (1811–20), when the Prince Regent (later to become George IV) commissioned the Brighton Pavilion. Filled with Chinese-style furniture and decorative and structural features, notably the

Above: Featuring small hand-painted scenes in the Chinese style, this red japanned bureau bookcase, with ball and claw feet, was made and painted in England in 1700.

superb cast-iron, stylized, *faux* bamboo bannisters, it marked the beginning of a trend for *faux* bamboo, which was often simulated on the light rattan chairs designed to furnish fashionable conservatories.

THE HEYDAY OF ENGLISH PAINTED FURNITURE

Many famous eighteenth century English cabinet makers and architects favoured painted furniture. Thomas Chippendale created a style known as Chinese Chippendale, which included wardrobes and other pieces of furniture featuring delicate Chinese landscapes and other scenes set against a light-coloured japanned background. Similarly, George Hepplewhite included many examples of painted furniture in his catalogue. And at the end of the century, Thomas Sheraton advocated japanned and other types of painted furniture in his *'Cabinet Directory'* of 1803 – particularly recommending the use of white, Prussian blue, vermilion and gray-green colours.

The first interior designer, architect Robert Adam (1728–92), commissioned painted furniture appropriate to his style of decor. As an advocate of the neo-classical look that developed during the 1760s, he ordered classical painted motifs of wreaths, vines, fans and medallions. And it was not long before other architects and designers followed suit – providing drawings for the decoration of the walls, upholstery, panelling and furniture, so that each item became a co-ordinated part of their whole design.

By the mid-eighteenth century various changes in technique had taken place, with some cabinet makers and companies painting directly onto the wood, without varnishing the surface first; and often, pigment was being mixed with water and glue rather than varnish or lacquer.

French influence

Thomas Hope (1769–1831), another English champion of classicism, was strongly influenced by the work of two French architects and interior designers, Charles Percier and Pierre Fontaine. During the first fifteen years of the nineteenth century their Empire-style pieces featured classical motifs such as palm, laurel, oak and ivy leaves, and figures found in classical mythology – for they strove to 'imitate the spirit, principles and wisdom of antiquity' (1812 edition of their *Recueil des Decorations Interieures*). The strict militaristic feeling of this period in France was echoed by the

Above: This Robert Adam-style pier-glass and table, painted wedgwood blue, lined and decorated with classical motifs in white, can be found in the dining room at Saltram House, England. Opposite left: An exotic French empire daybed, embellished with decorative gilding and painted with imitation lapis inlay, made in France circa 1810.

13

severe shapes and sombre, imperial appearance of the furniture, and Napoleonic motifs of the bee, eagle, swan and lyre, which often adorned pieces.

THE HEYDAY OF ITALIAN PAINTED FURNITURE

No other craftsmen throughout Europe managed to imitate the flowing essence of natural marble in the way that the Venetians were able to. Many of the finest examples of lacquered furniture produced in Venice between 1720 and 1740 – especially chests of drawers – featured tops painted in *faux marbre*. As a result, imitation marble tops became very popular not only in Venice but in Genoa, Turin and other Italian cities as well.

But it was the second half of the eighteenth century that saw the most outstanding era of Venetian furniture design. Influenced by Chippendale's *Gentleman and Cabinet maker's Director (1754)*, much of the painted furniture displayed a lightness of touch. Sparingly gilded and bronzed, it often featured floral motifs. And the success of the style rapidly spread to the furniture makers of Medina, Parma, Piacenza and Cremona (and to a lesser degree, the cabinet makers of Spain and Portugal), who copied the Venetian craftsmen.

Above: This Italian parcel gilt and black painted console table, with faux marbre *top, dates from the late eighteenth century.*

Above: This japanned papier-mâché *English chair was made in the mid-nineteenth century, and can be seen in the Victoria and Albert Museum in London, England.*

PAPIER MACHE FURNITURE

Techniques for making furniture out of paper were developed in Persia and the Middle East in ancient times. However, *papier mâché* furniture did not reach Europe until the beginning of the eighteenth century, when it found its way into France.

By 1765, Frederick the Great had set up the first European *papier mâché* factory in Berlin. But it was in England that *papier mâché* furniture became most popular, largely because the malleability of the product allowed it to be manipulated into the highly ornate forms that were popular there throughout the nineteenth century. Thus, in 1793 Henry Clay set up business in Birmingham, where he mass-produced trays, chairs, dressing, gaming and sewing tables and even beds right up until the 1860s.

Papier mâché furniture also became popular in the USA, although not until the middle of the nineteenth century, when the first factory was opened in Connecticut.

All *papier mâché* furniture required painting, and some of the finest examples of japanning in dark lacquer with Chinese-style motifs can be seen on *papier mâché* furniture. Embellishments of flowers, country landscapes and animals were also painted, and the more extravagant examples featured gilding and mother-of-pearl inlays. Whatever the design, the piece would nearly always be finished by hand polishing, to produce a lustrous, glossy effect.

RUSTIC FOLK ART

In the Alps, Scandanavia, and the east coast of the United States a different kind of painted furniture evolved. The craftsmen in these areas painted and stencilled mainly floral motifs onto green, black, brown or white backgrounds. The rose was a particular favourite of the Alpine painters, although by the eighteenth century they were embellishing armoires and chests with landscape scenes, filled with a wide range of flowers, birds and other animals, and figural scenes, usually depicting a wedding or a scene from the Bible.

In Sweden, during the middle of the eighteenth century, Hans Erson Enman established a significant new style of decorative painting. Onto a maroon coloured background, he painted flower blossoms in a thin wash of blue or white. The wash was so light you could see the background through the blossoms, thereby creating a strange, three-dimensional effect. By the end of the century, the maroon ground favoured by Enman had been dropped by painters imitating his style, in favour of a blue or green one.

In America painted furniture blossomed in Pennsylvania from about 1750 to 1850, following the great influx of German-speaking peoples. Known as the Pennsylvanian Dutch (derived from 'Deutsch'), they brought with them their decorative folk arts, and adorned virtually every household object with floral motifs, baskets of fruit and many kinds of bird – much of this rural imagery being stencilled, using natural dyes. Specialist artisans travelled from settlement to settlement on the east coast, stopping at each to decorate walls, chairs, tables, clocks and picture frames, using their hand-cut stencils.

Above: This dower chest is part of the rustic tradition. From Jonestown Pennsylvania, USA, it was made out of pine in 1784, by Christian Saltzer. He painted it red with cream panels to provide a contrasting ground for the large floral motifs.

THE DECLINE OF PAINTED FURNITURE

Factory-made furniture of the Victorian age emulated many styles, including classical, rococo and baroque. However, mass production meant that quality suffered and painted furniture lost its popularity.

There were some attempts at a revival – as a reaction to the poor, imitative factory furniture, William Morris set up a company that crafted furniture by hand, and sometimes decorated it lavishly with painted designs. And designers supporting Morris joined with him in the 1870s to form the Arts and Crafts Movement; out of which grew the sweeping curves, flowing lines and rounded shapes of the Art Nouveau style. Practitioners of this movement often employed freehand and stencil-painted motifs on furniture. For example, the innovative architect and designer Charles Rennie Mackintosh and his colleagues of the 'Glasgow Four' produced tall-backed chairs and co-ordinating wall banners depicting stylized figures entwined in roses.

However, the Arts and Crafts Movement was not enough to save painted furniture, and by the end of the nineteenth century it was no longer fashionable.

SMALL-SCALE REVIVALS

Although painted furniture fell from favour, it did not die out altogether. There have been a few notable revivals during the twentieth century The first began in 1913 when English art critic and painter Roger Fry, along with Vanessa Bell and Duncan Grant – fellow artists from a group of London-based intellectuals now known as the Bloomsbury group – established the Omega workshops.

Founded on the aesthetic principle that the decorative arts should draw their inspiration from the fine arts, the Omega workshop members became the first group of serious designers for many years to practice the art of painting furniture. All of the household objects they produced, including textiles and pottery as well as furniture, were decorated with simple, and often vividly coloured designs.

Unfortunately, the workshops were closed by 1920, but many of the best ideas found their way to Charleston, a Sussex farmhouse taken as a holiday home by Bell and Grant, which survives to this day. Almost the whole of its interior is decorated with paint; including walls, doors, baths, radiators, screens, mirror frames and lamps and much of the furniture – for example, many of the chairs are painted red, in an imitation of lacquer.

RECENT DEVELOPMENTS

The last decade has seen a resurgence of colour and ornament. Once again broken colour techniques are being experimented with. *Faux marbre* and wood-graining are gaining in popularity, and furniture with floral and character motifs painted on stippled and sponged backgrounds is sought after and collectable. All the signs point to a major revival in the art of painting furniture, and, with the aid of this book, you will be able to play a part in it.

Above: The tall, white-painted, free-standing wardrobe is by Charles Rennie Mackintosh. It contrasts in colour but not in style with the high-backed Mackintosh chair. Both are elegant, with just a hint of Art Nouveau, and could almost be modern pieces. They are to be found at Hill House, Helensburgh, Scotland; a house Mackintosh designed for the family of the Glasgow publisher Blackie. Opposite right: Hand-painted in an impressionistic Bloomsbury spirit, this chest of drawers, from Charleston, England, features dense curvaceous forms in muted shades of blues, greens and lilacs.

LIVING ROOMS

There are two basic types of living room: those furnished and decorated in a formal style, and used for special family occasions and entertaining guests; and more informal settings, used for family activities such as watching TV, reading, listening to music and generally relaxing in. However, in many of today's houses both formal and informal functions have to be catered for in a single room.

TRADITIONAL LIVING AREAS

If you have a separate reception room set aside for entertaining, or if you wish to decorate your sole living room in a formal style (only advisable if there are no young children in the household!), you could use antique-style painted furniture to create a traditional look.

Typical effects include the Chinoiserie style (see pages 8-10), which is based on lacquering, and is ideal for small tables, firescreens and mirror frames. The wood-graining (see page 22) of soft woods to imitate the more expensive hardwoods has long been practised – most pine bookcases were intended for this type of finish. However, different woods were in favour at different times, so if you are concerned to recreate an authentic period look, research carefully before opting for any particular type. Similarly, marbling (see page 14) has a history of use for items like table-tops, lamp bases and grand chiffoniers and cabinets.

Right: An elegant Directoire-style chair sits next to a more robust-looking chest of drawers, or commode. The golden borders and pale green scrolling of the commode blend perfectly with the sophisticated painted screen behind, and the faded rug on which it stands. The golden candlesticks are in keeping with the opulent air of this drawing room. Above: The Swedish-style settee, circular table and chair are all painted in a plain cream colour, which lends an air of quiet elegance to the room. (A recipe for a Swedish-style paint glaze is given on page 123.)

*Above: The trelliswork on the back of this occasional chair complements the cane
seat, and to provide a beautiful frame for the idyllic-looking, Italian renaissance child
in swaddling clothes (putto) depicted in the oval centre (see detail above).*

$\mathscr{C}$ONTEMPORARY LIVING AREAS

The simple lines of modern furniture are very suitable for the application of a wide range of paint techniques: spattered primary colours over white-painted tables and bookcases would create a bright and youthful look; or substitute marbling over the same base and you will achieve an elegant and sophisticated Italian style.

However, the pieces chosen for painting don't have to be new. Inexpensive items that have seen better days can be transformed very cheaply with paint – making them ideal for those on a low budget. And broadly speaking, suitable techniques for a modern look, such as sponging, ragging, spattering and stippling, are much easier to execute than those required to create a traditional look, like gilding or graining. So, a modern theme can be a wise choice for those new to decorative painting.

Above: This matt black painted large table, which has another role as one half of a double bed base, pulls together all the different pastel grey and cream surfaces in the large, square room, which features only Japanese-style contemporary furniture made from natural materials.

COUNTRY STYLE LIVING AREAS

A country style can be either modern or traditional, or bridge the gap between the two. For example, you can use sponging and stencilling in soft, natural colours to link a rustic period pine table with a modern hi-fi unit, so that they both blend into their surroundings.

The essence of a country look is busy harmony. And one way of achieving this is to copy motifs from the wallpaper or curtain fabric and stencil them onto the painted or bare wood furniture. As always, the important thing is knowing when to stop – overdo the decorations and all you'll create is a mess.

Opposite right: Cressida Bell painted this Charleston-influenced room (see pages 16–7), using bold blues, yellows and pinks. The blue and pink repeating pattern on the wall was achieved by dabbing with a synthetic sponge cut in the simple crude shape of a leaf. Although the room is filled with pattern and colour, it is not overwhelming because each piece is imbued with the same generous spirit, optimistic style and strength of colour. Above: Cressida painted huge voluptuous urns on either side of the fireplace, and created a three-dimensional pattern along the edge of the mantelpiece, again using yellow and blue, as well as black to simulate shade – a bold feature totally in keeping with the rest of the room.

PROJECT ONE

CHERUB CHAIR

My Queen Anne drawing room was in need of another occasional chair – one that would be both functional and fit into the surrounding decor. So, having acquired an ordinary, and relatively inexpensive, Spanish whitewood chair with a cane seat, I asked artist Nessa Kearney to 'transform' it into an elegant, eighteenth-century, Sheraton-style chair.

1, 2 & 3 *Having first prepared the surface (see page 118), Nessa Kearney 'aged' the chair, by sponging it (see page 127) with a mushroom gray eggshell paint – a colour found in the classical eighteenth-century French design reproduced at intervals on the walls. Instantly the chair took on a more delicate, almost fragile appearance. When the glaze had dried, she lined its edges in a dark blue (see page 144) – echoing the predominant colour of the walls.*

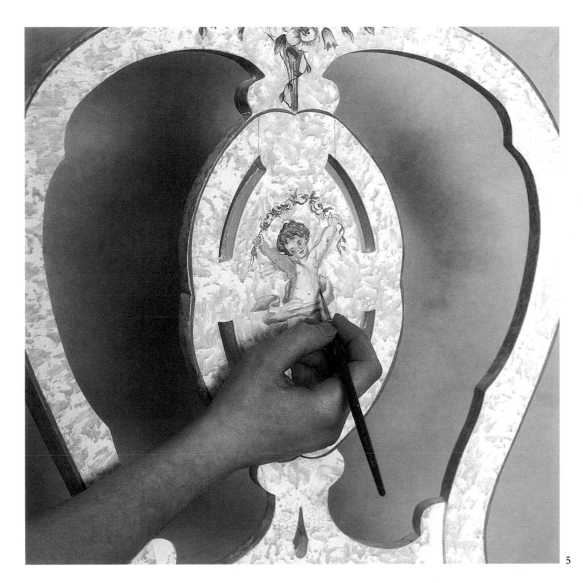

5

4 & 5 *To establish the chair as eighteenth century,
Nessa embellished the back with a cherub. Having
drawn the outline onto tracing paper (you could trace
the figure from an art book), she placed this over a sheet
of supercharged, waxless carbon paper (available from
artists' suppliers), fixed both of them in position on the
back of the chair with masking tape, and transferred the
outline by rubbing over the paper with a hard 4H pencil.
Nessa then painted in the cherub using a fine artists'
sable brush and enamel paints.*

6 *Nessa used colours to reflect those found in the late eighteenth-century Aubisson rug lying on the floor next to the chair. And she added neo-classical floral decorations freehand, highlighting the blue ribbon and flower garland, before applying the finishing touches to the cherub — shading the figure, to give it a three-dimensional quality and 'life'.*
7 *Whilst the finished chair would sit well in almost any room that contained antique furniture, it is especially successful in my drawing room. This is because both the classical and floral motifs and the colours used are drawn from the surrounding decor — notably the walls and rug. Thus the chair, whilst retaining its own individual shape and character, is in harmony with the rest of the room.*

FITTED FURNITURE

Built-in furniture is a great space saver, and may be the only way of storing and displaying functional and decorative objects in the small living room of a modern house. If this is the case it is a good idea to make larger pieces, such as the cupboards in alcoves on either side of a fireplace, seem less obtrusive by painting them in the same colour as the surrounding walls. However, in a larger room, where a sense of space is not a problem, you can draw attention to fitted items either by flat painting them in bold or contrasting colours, or by trying out some of the many broken colour effects described in the Techniques chapter (see pages 127–57).

Above: Row upon row of drab-looking books, sitting on these bookshelves in Clive Bell's house in London, England, were cheered-up immeasurably by a simple pattern being painted, by Duncan Grant, down each vertical and along the top edge of the bookcase. Duncan added a final flourish by painting a pair of figures playing guitars onto the two square cupboards at the bottom of the shelves.
Left: From the real to the imaginary, the books, and even the seashell, in these faux marbre *fitted cupboards are entirely a work of* trompe l'oeil, *by Paul Treadaway.*
Opposite right: This series of sculptured post-modern bookcases, by Charles Jencks, was wood-grained (see page 142) to give a sense of solidity, and then lined (see page 145) to emphasize the strong shape and form.

CHAIRS AND SOFAS

You should not shy away from painting uphol-stered furniture, as even the most dull and ordinary pieces can be transformed into seeming-ly valuable 'antiques' by delicately painting the wooden arms and legs – especially if they are then lined in the classical manner.

Even fabric-covered sofas may offer scope for painting – for example, the wooden bun feet of a Chesterfield settee could be sponged in two of the upholstery colours.

Similarly, try wood-graining (see page 22) wooden-framed chairs and settees in a finish that complements the close cover fabric. The pieces need not be part of a matching suite – if you use the same paint technique (see page 20), you can link together an odd collection of pieces to create a co-ordinated look.

Above: Greens, pinks and cream colours were painted onto the frame of this sofa, to complement the delicate patterning of the rug covering it.

$\mathscr{O}$CCASIONAL TABLES

Coffee tables, nests of tables and side tables are but three examples of the many different types of occasional table found in the living room. Being relatively small pieces of furniture, painting one is an appropriate project for someone new to the use of broken colour techniques.

The type of finish you choose will depend on the surrounding decor. For example, in a cottage-style interior a delicate stencilled floral border around a table top, on top of a pale-coloured base coat, is effective. While a bright primary-spattered table will inject a dash of colour into a modern, neutral-coloured setting. And a wood-grained finish (see page 22) that matches another piece in the room, such as a chair, bureau or desk, would be the most appropriate finish in a traditional interior.

Above: This modern-looking coffee table was made to look less solid by stippling the sides in blue and then stencilling simple floral motifs around the top edge (see page 136).

$\mathscr{S}$TORAGE FURNITURE

Provided you have the space, free-standing cupboards tend to look better in country-style living rooms than their built-in counterparts do. Moreover, a dragged finish will make even the largest of cupboards look more elegant – especially if the panels and doors are highlighted with lining. Alternatively, an integrated and less formal effect can be achieved by stippling on the base coat and then, in a contrasting colour, decorating on top with hand-painted or stencilled motifs taken from the curtain or upholstery fabric used in the room.

In a more formal and traditional urban setting, lacquering a small, table-mounted cabinet will provide an elegant addition to the decor.

Above: This grand eighteenth-century cupboard was looking somewhat the worse for wear before Hannerley Dehn stripped it (see page 119), and applied a creamy brown ragged finish (see page 130). She then defined the panels, drawers and the majestic cornice by lining them in blue (see page 145). Hannerley reinforced the elegant Empire style by adding some ribbons and painting two classical urns encircled by laurel leaves within the panels. Opposite right: The natural-looking chest of drawers with a pink marble top was actually painted with a ragged (see page 130) and antiqued (see page 148) finish, under the green leaves and pink flowers.

Fireplaces

Think carefully before painting a fireplace, as its size and position can make a huge impact on the style and atmosphere of a living room. If you wish to make the fireplace a focal point, try a striking, opulent effect such as *faux marbre* or even a bold, hand-painted effect (see pages 24-5) or an abstract design, using a combination of techniques such as spattering and ragging. If you do not have a fireplace, why not paint a *trompe l'oeil* one on the wall – fire basket, burning coals, marble surround and all.

And don't forget fire accessories, such as coal scuttles, fenders and firescreens. They lend themselves to any number of painted finishes – though wood-graining, lacquering and *trompe l'oeil* are particularly appropriate.

Above: The strong form of this Charles Jencks fireplace was made to look even more solid by the addition of a rich red faux marbre *finish. Above the fireplace, supporting the imposing bust, is a plinth, also given a* faux marbre *finish – this time in dramatic black and orange.*

Left: This charming country cottage fire surround, made from pine, was stencilled with a simple rustic red and green flower and leaf design (see page 136). Below: This fireplace can be found in the drawing room at Charleston, England (see page 16). Painted in the 1930s by Duncan Grant, the figures on either side have a voluptuous, lively quality – being executed in the flamboyant manner characteristic of the artist.

$\mathscr{D}$ESKS

All kinds of desks – roll-tops, bureaux and plain planks of chipboard with trestle supports, to name but a few – can be given an often necessary touch of originality and style with an appropriate paint technique.

If you are short of cash, consider transforming a discarded piece of office furniture. For example, a roll-top office desk can be softened by decorating the sides and legs with flowing *trompe l'oeil* ribbons, and stencilling a small motif on each of the tiny drawers that are revealed when the top is rolled back. And to make a rectangular table-style desk look elegant, sponge it then apply fine or edge lining to the top and drawers. Co-ordination is important – if you intend to stencil a motif onto a desk try to take it from fabric or furnishings elsewhere in the room.

Above left: The surfaces of this modern work station were spattered (see page 132) silver on a dark blue background (thus picking up the colour of the blinds) for a striking, hi-tech effect. The old-fashioned typewriter was given a similar treatment. Above right: By way of comparison, this traditional-style desk looks quite sombre. The exterior was dragged in cream (see page 128), while the inside was painted to match the chair.

$\mathcal{S}$MALL PIECES

In almost any setting you will find small objects that are suitable for some of the more elaborate paint techniques which might prove too bold or overbearing on larger items. For example, clocks and picture or mirror frames can be featured by painting a tortoiseshell effect on the frame or surround. Or, if the room has a very modern decor, use a spattered finish, or a bold fantasy effect, such as marbling.

Similarly, cigarette and other small boxes lend themselves to tortoiseshelling, wood-graining, lacquering and almost any fantasy finish you might care to think of.

Finally, for an integrated look, waste-paper baskets should be painted in a colour to complement the rest of the furniture, regardless of the finish that you use.

Above: This sophisticated-looking, small circular table was painted black and then lined (see page 145) and decorated in gold around the top and down the curved legs. In the centre of the table delicate carnations were painted, to echo Victorian papier mâché *furniture (see page 14).*

$\mathcal{K}$ITCHENS AND DINING ROOMS

Fast returning to its original position as the heart of the home, the kitchen (and the kitchen/diner, where meals are eaten as well as prepared) ought to be a stylish, welcoming and comfortable setting, in addition to being an efficient workplace. Exactly the same principles should be applied when choosing the decor and furnishings in a separate dining room – though given guests may be entertained there, greater emphasis should be placed on formality rather than function.

MODERN FITTED KITCHENS

With space at a premium in most homes today, kitchens and kitchen/diners occupy only a relatively small area – given that they have to cater for the storage of food, cooking utensils and china, as well as cooking, eating, washing-up and even entertaining.

The subsequent pressure on the space has resulted in the fitted kitchen – an ergonomically efficient system of storage cupboards, worktops and appliances. Whilst it is possible to buy a fitted kitchen relatively cheaply, if you want especially elegant or individual fittings you usually have to find a substantial amount of money.

However, with careful use of a variety of paint techniques, you can redecorate your old, tatty and somewhat anonymous fitted kitchen. If you paint the cupboards to co-ordinate with the walls and floor you will create a sophisticated, stylish and seemingly spacious setting for little more than the cost of the paints.

Kitchen units can be painted in virtually any of the broken colour finishes detailed on pages 127–151. Marbled, dragged and lined units and worktops will produce a sophisticated almost opulent look, whilst sponged, ragged, stippled and spattered finishes, in soft pastel colours, will add a quiet elegance and increase the sense of space – especially if the effect is continued onto the table and chairs. To see the spectacular effect of a *trompe l'oeil* mural over fitted kitchen units turn to pages 46–51.

And broken colour techniques applied in primary colours will add freshness and a feeling of uplift. Whilst the simple contrast of black units, table and chairs against white worktop, tiles and floor, will produce a very chic look.

Above: Although this modern galley kitchen is narrow, there is an abundance of natural light. This has allowed the artist to use gray as the main base colour for the units, without it seeming oppressive. The blues and yellows in the flamboyant abstract motifs provide a striking contrast, and help to break up the angular shape of the layout and create a greater sense of space.

*Above: Another example of a kitchen where the artist
has used paint to make a bold statement. However, in
this case only plain colours have been used, and in
carefully controlled blocks – squares, rectangles,
diamonds and triangles. The result is a more formal
style than the kitchen opposite, but it is
nonetheless effective.*

COUNTRY STYLE KITCHENS

The advantages of broken colour techniques are not confined to modern fitted kitchens; traditional country style kitchens, containing separate dressers, tables and appliances, can also be transformed into elegant interiors.

The secret is to use soft pastel glazes and washes on the furniture; or simply strip back to the bare wood and varnish. But in either case, it is appropriate to stencil motifs such as baskets of fruit and garlands of flowers on top – preferably designs that are incorporated in fabrics such as the tablecloth and curtains. Stencilled borders around table-tops and cupboard doors look especially effective, and whilst earthy colours should be used most of the time, the odd splash of primary colour will brighten things up.

An unfitted kitchen featuring individual pieces of furniture – such as a dresser, individual cupboards, tables and shelves, together with a free-standing stove – will benefit from one paint finish such as dragging being applied in a single colour to all the disparate elements. This will have the effect of co-ordinating them without destroying their individuality, increasing the sense of space and lending an air of greater efficiency. This effect can be accentuated by displaying some patterned china and copying the motif onto the furniture by stencil.

Above: Charm and rustic simplicity are the key to this homely-looking country kitchen – painted motifs have been applied with restraint, so as not to spoil the natural, unsophisticated look. In pride of place is the large oak dresser. The graceful, curving edge carved along the top, overhanging panel is echoed by the shape of the simple, two-colour floral motif painted above it, and on the drawers – which were also lined in blue. The same motif was painted onto the backs of the kitchen chairs, to create a subtly co-ordinated look.

$\mathscr{D}$INING ROOMS

Quite simply, if you have a combined kitchen/ diner, decorate both sections, in whatever style you choose, to co-ordinate or complement each other – and this refers to paint effects as well as colours. Don't create a full-blown country kitchen at one end of the room and a quasi-oriental modern dining area at the other!

As separate dining rooms are cut off from the kitchen, they tend to have a more intimate and formal atmosphere than combined dining areas. Separated from such functions as the preparation of food and washing-up, and being part of the home where guests are entertained, they should be stylishly decorated and furnished. You can create the appropriate look with techniques such as dark wood-graining, lacquering and gilding – effects that might look too formal and somewhat overstated in the steam of a kitchen.

Ultimately, the use of such techniques in combination with rich, dark colours like red and green, for example, will create a cosy and intimate atmosphere.

Above: This elegant dining room breathes sophistication in its restrained use of colour and uncluttered appearance. The blue-gray painted dining-room chairs and dresser echo the delicate blue pattern on the wall, and highlight the glossy white, circular dining table, with its delicately carved edging. The large wall mirror, which reflects the table, makes this spacious room seem even larger and lighter than it really is.

TROMPE L'OEIL KITCHEN

I felt that my bright modern kitchen, although very smart, lacked warmth and seemed somewhat impersonal. I hankered after a much more lively and homely style that was a truer reflection of my personality. So, I decided to paint the units a warm yellow to match the walls, and then asked an artist, Tony Raymond, to come up with some ideas for painting a *trompe l'oeil* on the cupboard doors. Perhaps the most important thing to remember when attempting to portray a number of *trompe l'oeil* images on a run of kitchen units, is that the successful appearance of each cupboard depends to some extent on the others. Consequently, it is essential to treat them all as one painting.

1 *Tony took a close look at the original kitchen, and decided that the open wall cupboard used to display vases and jars should set the style for the* trompe l'oeil.
2 *Having carefully keyed the surface to take a paint finish (see page 119), the units were painted with a warm, sunny yellow eggshell glaze.*

3 *A white glaze was sponged on top of the yellow
finish (see page 127), to lighten the overall effect.*
4 *Tony showed me his pencil and colour roughs for
approval. (Sketches are always good for giving an idea
of the finished product before you start in earnest, and
for reference whilst you work.)* 5 *When the glaze had
dried, Tony began to sketch the outline of the* trompe
l'oeil *shelving and objects onto the units, with a pencil.
(Getting the perspective right is crucial, and is affected
by the height from which the object is viewed – the
average eye-level is 158 cm (5 ft 3 in) – bear this in
mind, and step back constantly to review the angle of
the lines.)* 6 *Taking one cupboard at a time, Tony
blocked in each of the objects depicted, using white
acrylic paint.*

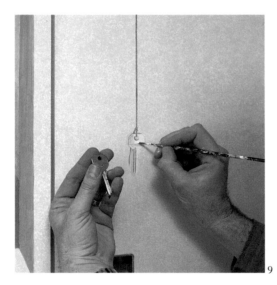

7 *Onto one of the cupboard doors Tony painted in the details on top of the blocked-in outlines of a postcard and a small calendar.* **8** *He then added a drawing pin and a length of blue string.* **9** *At the end of the string he 'hung' a door key. (Note how the addition of darker and lighter toned glazes, that is, shading and highlights, begins to establish the appearance of three-dimensions.)* **10** *On this door depicting open shelving and vases Tony, having tentatively defined the shadows cast by the predominant light source playing across their surface (he used a very thin wash of red ochre), began building up the detail on the objects with a fine sable brush.*

11 *Tony picked out the fruit on the lower shelf, then built up the shading on the leaves spilling out of the vases, and on the cloth and glasses in the basket. The darker glaze applied in the corners represents the shadows cast by the objects, and thus underpins the sense of three-dimensions.* **12** *On this shelf, Tony painted a chinoiserie vase, a book and some dried flowers. Again, it is the shading, as well as the high quality artwork, that creates the 3-D effect.* **13** *Tony moved between cupboards, gradually building up detail, modifying the design, and deepening the shadows. He added some appropriate lettering on the spine of the book, as well as the wrapper of my favourite chocolate bar hanging over the edge of the shelf.* **14** *After surveying the whole effect, he strengthened the shadows and highlights on and around the flowers, to increase their definition.*

15

15 *As a finishing touch, Tony depicted a*
much loved item of mine: a Dragon's teddy.
Copied exactly from the original, the teddy
has a sad air, although he looks well cared
for judging by the state of his fur. Tony
added highlight to the eyes – which are,
after all, made of glass. 16 *Finally, when*
Tony was satisfied with all the details,
shadows and highlights, and when the paint
had dried, he gave the cupboards two coats
of clear polyurethane varnish, to protect his
beautiful illusion; a masterly example of
trompe l'oeil.
If you wish to try this striking paint
technique for yourself, additional
information, and a simpler project to try as a
first attempt, can be found in the section on
pages 156–7.

16

KITCHEN UNITS

Fitted kitchen cupboards that are beginning to look a bit jaded provide ideal surfaces for broken colour techniques, especially stencilling (see page 136), as the doors are often flat and of roughly the same size.

Hand-painted or stencilled borders on each panel will define the shape of the units and give them greater presence, and repeated motifs, such as baskets of fruit or flowers, will help to establish a country cottage style without distracting from the fitted feel.

Of course, there is nothing to stop you using any of the broken colour techniques on kitchen units. Try marbling or sponging for a cool, fresh setting, lacquering or dragging and lining for sophisticated urban chic or even an abstract mural, painted freehand, to create a truly individual look (see page 42).

Above: Painted in the Venetian style, this sophisticated fitted kitchen features white marble worktops and wall tiles. The panels of the units were given a complementary faux marbre finish, while the frame surrounds were dragged in green. The finishing touch in this elegant setting is provided by the classical urn containing pink flowers, painted on the white tiles. Right: Decorated entirely in wedgwood blue and white, this country kitchen has a French look about it. All the woodwork was dragged (see page 128), and the use of a single colour, blue, meant that different patterns – stripes on the walls, checks on the tablecloth, and dots on the tiles and worktop – could be successfully combined.

Dressers

Dressers are often found in country kitchens, accompanied by a large oak or pine refectory table and flagstones or quarry tiles on the floor (see page 44). In such a setting, the best treatment is to stipple on a base coat in a natural colour like green or brown, and then add floral borders within the panels, using subdued 'rustic' colours, such as dark red or pale yellow. Emphasise edges by lining them, and add sprigs of fruit along the shelves and in the centre of the panels. Alternatively, dressers can be given a more sophisticated look by using techniques like marbling or lacquering.

Above: The rich red-coloured back of this impressive-looking antique dresser is the perfect foil for the delicate porcelain figures and bright plates displayed on it. The green-blue painted wood surround complements the back, and the gold lining adds an air of sophistication, and echoes the gold-painted, Chinese-inspired motifs of ferns, pagodas and boats. Opposite right: By way of contrast, this dresser has been painted in black and white, and displays a black and white dinner service to complete the co-ordinated effect. The surrounds were dragged (see page 128), the drawers marbled and outlined in white, and a panel on each side was combed (see page 129) to contrast with the dragged background. The light brown worktop serves to highlight the elegance of this dresser.

STORAGE FURNITURE

If you have a sideboard made from a light-hued wood, such as maple or pine, but would prefer a more traditional and formal look, try dragging it in a rich dark brown colour. Alternatively, use a graining technique to produce an imitation walnut or rosewood finish – but do make sure that it matches the dining table.

Providing the sideboard has clean and simple lines, and is not covered with ornate panelling and elaborate mouldings, a lacquered finish will look elegant in traditional and modern settings.

In country kitchens or dining rooms large storage cupboards can be made more attractive by dragging and lining the framework and doors.

Above left: Painted in coral, dark blue and lilac colours, this dresser has tremendous presence. The painted papier-mâché *pygmies supporting the shelf, and the figures of Neptune and the mermaid, add to the outlandish nature of the piece – which relates so effectively to the curtains over the window, the dark blue frieze on the ceiling and the extravagant chandelier over the dining table. In any other setting it might look rather gaudy. Above right: By way of contrast, this sideboard has been given an elegant finish, and would sit happily in many interiors. Opposite right: This substantial cupboard has been made less overbearing by antiquing it. The sides, cornice and arched panels on the doors have been ragged (see page 130) in turquoise, to accentuate the height; whilst the drawers below have been ragged with a combination of the turquoise and a light brown, to produce a mottled effect. With the addition of swirling hand-painted motifs (see page 136), the result is one of elegant faded grandeur.*

CHAIRS AND STOOLS

Simple kitchen chairs or breakfast bar stools look good with a character or flower motif painted freehand or stencilled on the top, especially in a country-style setting. You might even try bambooing the legs (see page 10).

On the other hand, if you have painted the kitchen units with one of the broken colour techniques, such as marbling, wood-graining or stippling, create a co-ordinated look by matching stools or plain kitchen chairs in the same colour and style.

In a dining area the arms, legs and backs of chairs with upholstered seats call for a more formal painted effect, such as wood-graining, sophisticated hand-painted motifs (see page 45) or lining. For a slightly off-beat but stylish look, you could choose a colour that complements the upholstery fabric, rather than simulating the hue of a natural wood.

Above: In this homely cottage kitchen both the stool and writing desk have been given a dragged (see page 128), antiqued finish in country green. Even the plant pots have been painted, with lively and colourful flower motifs. Left: After first colourwashing it in light blue (see page 133), the delicate curves of this charming chair were accentuated by lining (see page 145) in blue, and blocking in the central motif with the same complementary colour. Opposite right: The simple, country-style chairs in this kitchen-diner were painted a pastel green, to match the ragged green storage units (see page 130) – colours picked up in the bold, green and red painted flower on the wall, and in the floral design on the wooden floor.

TABLES

Pine kitchen tables in a country-style kitchen should be decorated with painted motifs. On a large table, paint or stencil a border first; then add a large central motif, such as a basket of flowers. Dining tables can be decorated with floral motifs too (see page 40).

However, you may feel that painted motifs will look out of place on a more formal dining-room table, where an imitation dark wood finish, such as walnut or mahogany, is appropriate. In a very grand dining room a lacquered table would look especially impressive.

Above: A fine example of skilful rosewood graining, by Hannerley Dehn, has turned this octagonal dining table into a convincing Regency antique. Having painstakingly built up the grain, using fine sable brushes and oil paints, Hannerley applied several coats of varnish, before waxing and polishing to achieve a deep, lustrous shine. Right: At first glance the distinctive, post-modernist, circular table and accompanying dining chairs, by Charles Jencks, do not appear to feature any paint finish. However, closer examination reveals that they have been given a pine wood-grain finish, and that the bold, curving shapes and rectangular slats have been emphasized by lining, in a dark brown.

$\mathcal{S}$MALL PIECES

Whatever style of kitchen or dining room you have, it will contain some small items that are suitable subjects for certain of the more colourful and striking paint finishes which might prove overbearing on larger pieces.

For example, if your room is modern and high-tech in style you could paint a trolley in matt black, or use a fantasy marble finish. Drinks trays look elegant painted with a black lacquer base coat and a chinoiserie design, in gold, on top. Alternatively, paint them a pretty pastel shade and add a whimsical floral border – it just depends on the surrounding decor.

Finally, don't forget that you can decorate the kitchen clock. Use any paint technique you like – stencilled or hand-painted motifs are my favourites – but pick up the colour from elsewhere in the room for a co-ordinated look.

Above left: This air-tight bread bin was painted a rich deep brown. Then, to create a rustic look, the artist first traced and then painted sunny yellow sheaves of corn around the sides of the bin and on the lid – adding the contents of the container in elaborate lettering. Above right: The colours and shapes of the floral motifs on this circular Victorian clock-face provided the inspiration for the luxuriant floral grouping on the top of the frame; whilst the red, yellow, green and blue colours were repeated on the four corners, but this time in a complementary abstract pattern. Opposite: Trays are ideal candidates for all manner of paint finishes, as in the collection here. From left to right: black provides the contrast for a very faint chinoiserie design; an extravagant grouping of flowers and a patterned edge float on a sea of black; a highly polished, plain black lacquer surface can look very elegant; black as an effective background for both an abstract design and a bouquet of flowers; a tray painted to resemble a chocolate box – a huge collage of flowers in subdued creams and browns, painted on a black background and encircled in gold; sophisticated figures encircled in black were painted onto this gold-spattered background.

ℬEDROOMS

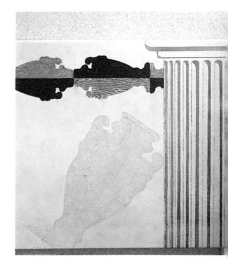

First and foremost a bedroom is a place to relax and unwind in, and somewhere to escape from the rest of the family, for a while. As such, the decor should express and complement your personality. And because, at the end of the day, it is only important if you like the style, you can experiment with a variety of finishes and be as idiosyncratic as you please.

ROMANTIC SETTINGS

Bedrooms are usually decorated in a romantic style to provide a stimulating escape from the often dreary monotony of everyday life. So, if the walls and floor are in warm, soft pastel shades it will be appropriate to extend both the colours and the finish (sponging and ragging are very effective) to furniture such as fitted wardrobes, the bedhead, free-standing dressers and the linen chest at the end of the bed. Then copy flower motifs from the wallpaper, curtains or bedspread, and hand paint or stencil them on top.

If you wish to take the escapist element of a romantic setting to its logical conclusion, there is nothing to stop you decorating the ceiling, walls, floor and furniture – free-standing or fitted – with an elaborate *trompe l'oeil* mural. For example, having painted the pillars of the temple of Aphrodite, set against a blue sky and green fields, onto the wall, you could extend the marbled effect to the furniture. The sheer density and weight of the real stone would preclude its use on many of the larger items (such as wardrobe doors), but that merely adds to the fantasy of the marbled finish.

Above: This sumptuous baroque-style bedroom owes much of its atmosphere to Althea Wilson's painted decoration on the side of the day bed, which echoes the large, English floral prints on the curtains and bedspreads. Opposite right: You can almost feel the English summer in this pretty, peaceful country style bedroom – an ambience achieved by the use of pastel colours and floral motifs.

In a simple rustic bedroom, you can create a country look by stencilling the wooden floor and running a stencilled border round the top of the walls. Then stencil the same motif(s) on the bedhead, bedposts and other simple bare wood or colourwashed pieces to add to the charm. Floral or naive hand-painted motifs can be used in the same way. If you paint the bed with motifs, take into account the pattern on the quilt or bedcover – it would be a shame if the two designs 'fought' each other. Instead, repeat the fabric design on the furniture – or the furniture design on the fabric.

If you prefer a plainer look, you will find that dragging the same soft colours over a hotch-potch collection of different-sized and styled pieces of furniture will co-ordinate them, and make the room look less cluttered – often a problem in small, cottage style bedrooms.

Above: The vase on the back of the door of Duncan Grant's bedroom, at Charleston, England (see page 16), was painted by Vanessa Bell in 1916, and was one of her favourite decorative motifs. She painted the bookcase too, in the distinctive yellows and blacks of the Omega period. The crudely stippled effect and large shapes are characteristic of her lively artistic style – which had no pretensions to a 'perfect', machine-like finish – and they lend a fresh, unsophisticated atmosphere to the rooms she decorated.

$\mathscr{P}$RACTICAL SETTINGS

For those who prefer a practical yet elegant bedroom – a setting that encourages you to get up and out of bed in the morning – light and airy colourwashed or stippled walls offset by 'antique' wood-grained and lined furniture, or lacquered pieces in a contrasting colour, or small items of *faux* bamboo, should provide the answer. Whereas for a quasi-oriental modern finish, paint the walls plain or off-white, lacquer all the furniture in black and add gilded chinoiserie-style motifs on top. This style is well suited to modern, low-ceilinged rooms.

Whatever the decor in your bedroom, by painting the furniture to co-ordinate with or complement the surroundings, you will increase the sense of space and style, and as a result you might find yourself escaping there more and more often!

Above: This highly practical, co-ordinated bedroom was designed and decorated by Wesley Barrell. The long run of fitted cupboards – which might otherwise have been quite overbearing – were dragged in a dusky pink colour (see page 128), and the panels rag-rolled in pink on white (see page 130). The pastel green curtains in the cupboard windows provide an effective contrast to the pink and white, whilst linking the cupboards with the green quilted bedspread.

PROJECT THREE

ORIENTAL HEADBOARD

The decor of my attic bedroom (see page 72) had a slightly Eastern flavour and a quiet air of opulence about it. Qualities underpinned by the predominant shades of pink and red on the ceiling, walls and bedside tables, and by the arabesques featured on the sumptuous-looking bedspread. I wanted the bedhead, made from plain, off-white MDF (medium density fibreboard), to harmonize with the rest of the interior, whilst remaining a feature in its own right, and thus asked artist Nessa Kearney to decorate it in an appropriate style.

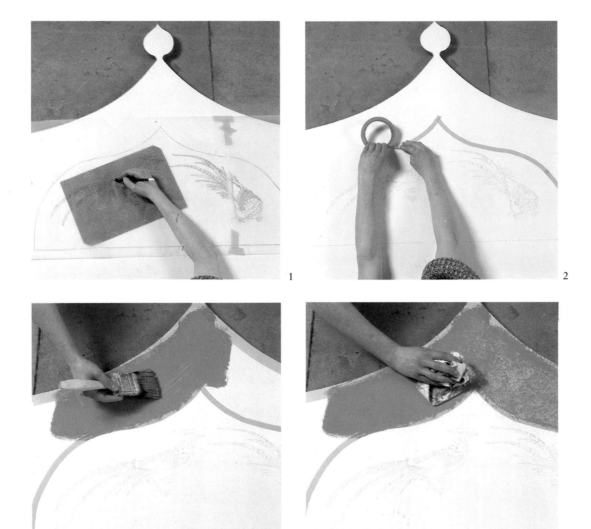

1 *To echo the peacock eyes featured on the fabric covering the walls, Nessa Kearney traced the outlines of two peacocks from a picture, and then used a sheet of supercharged, waxless carbon paper to transfer them to within the outline of a minaret dome which echoed the shape of the curved headboard.* **2 & 3** *She then masked off the top edge of the headboard and the outline of the dome. Next she applied a deep pink eggshell glaze to the area in between the tape.* **4** *Nessa ragged the pink glaze (see page 130) to produce a mottled finish.*

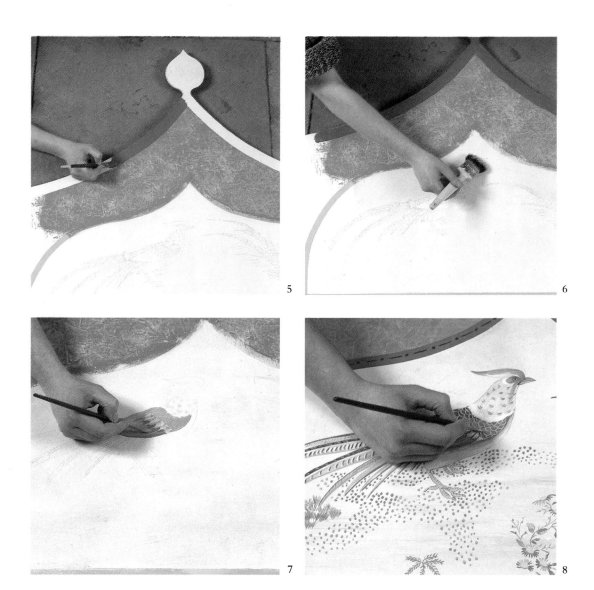

5 *When the glaze had dried, Nessa removed the masking tape from the top edge of the headboard, and filled in a border of deep pinky-red glaze.* **6** *She then painted in the dome shape, above and below the birds, in white – dabbing off any wet glaze from the motifs with crumpled kitchen paper – before removing the masking tape and brushing in a thin deep pinky-red outline to match the top edge.* **7** *Beginning with the light blue body and the darker wing feathers, Nessa began painting in the bird motifs.* **8** *She coloured their necks cream and breasts pink, and added long brown feathers and cream scallops to the blue bodies. And she grounded the birds by adding little groupings of seeds, leaves and flowers, as in a naive painting.*

9

10

9 *Nessa applied darker patches of glaze to the birds' necks, and deepened some of the colours elsewhere on their bodies and in the flowers and leaves, in order to introduce an element of shading, and therefore three-dimensions, to the scene.* 10 *She applied the finishing touches by adding a dot and line pattern to the centre of the dome border; ragging and lining (see pages 130 and 145) the bedhead uprights, and painting a series of arabesques, in blue and deep pinky-red, over the bed knobs.* 11 *On the finished bedhead, the two birds stand out clearly against the white and mottled pink background. And just as I had wanted, the bedhead has become both a feature and an harmonious part of this exotic interior.*

11

BEDS

Beds come in all shapes and sizes, and lend themselves to various paint techniques – the choice of which partly depends on the surrounding decor. For example, a large, elegant bed with an elaborate headboard and end panel can look spectacular in an Oriental-style setting when painted in rich red and gold colours. You should accentuate any curves by lining them and embellishing with arabesques (see pages 70-3).

On the other hand, on a romantic four-poster draped with voile or net, and set in a bedroom decorated in a traditional, country-house style, hand-paint or stencil delicate garlands of flowers on the frame (see page 92).

Less stately and more modern beds in simpler surroundings can also be stencilled. Or try tortoiseshelling or lacquering the headboard and end panel; or even applying a fantasy finish (see page 64) for a cool classical look.

When painting the bed, take into account the quilt or bedcover – the two designs must harmonize, not fight one another. With a patterned cover, the simplest approach is to repeat part of the fabric design on the bed.

Above: The gray and white combination, on the bedcover and headboard, provides a subtle contrast with the red in the abstract design on the wall. Opposite right (top): Green and brown – the colours of the countryside – are used on this attractive bedhead. The naive motif on the bed linen harmonizes with the stencilled chair. Opposite right (bottom): This modern bedroom is unified by the simple use of colour – the bedhead and cupboard are painted in the same pretty pastel colours as the curtains.

$\mathscr{S}$TORAGE FURNITURE

Free-standing wardrobes should complement rather than blend into the walls. The best way to achieve this is to paint them both the same colour, but use a different finish on each. For example, you could drag (see page 69) the wardrobe, and stipple or sponge the walls. Then line the panels and drawers, or stencil them with motifs that are taken from fabrics elsewhere in the room, such as the curtains or bedspread. You will discover that painting such large, solid pieces of furniture in this manner will make them seem lighter and more attractive.

Chests of drawers and blanket boxes often look rather cumbersome without decoration.

You can lighten such pieces by dragging or stippling them in pastel shades that complement the predominant colour of the room. And finish off by hand-painting or stencilling (see page 67) the drawers with flowers, for example.

Alternatively, small chests can look spectacular, whether they are in a modern or a traditional setting, if they are lacquered and embellished with small motifs. And dressing tables, generally more delicate pieces, are suitable for colour-washing and lining (see page 67) and wood-graining. Though if the room is big enough and you have already marbled the bed, you could decorate the dressing table to match.

*Above: A romantic effect was achieved by decorating
this chest of drawers with a pastel lilac-blue wash –
thereby providing an eye-catching contrast to
the gold handles.*

*Above (top): The dressing table was dragged in pale
blue (see page 128), and lined in a darker tone (see
page 145). A simple green and pink floral motif was
then traced onto each drawer (and the adjacent chair).
Above: The chest of drawers was wood-grained, and
then lined for added sophistication.*

FITTED FURNITURE

Many modern bedrooms feature a run of floor-to-ceiling, built-in cupboards, along one wall. Although wonderful for storage, these units can easily overpower a room if decorated too boldly. Therefore you should either make them blend into the background by painting them the same colour as the surrounding walls (see page 16), perhaps using a technique such as ragging or sponging on both surfaces (see page 69); or, if you do wish to paint them a different colour, stick to soft, pastel shades and use delicate sponging and stencilling techniques (see page 80).

Above: These fitted cupboards have a quiet, modern sophistication about them. Neatly broken up by the windows and curtains behind, they have dragged white surrounds (see page 128) with yellow ragged panels (see page 130), lined with a deeper yellow (see page 145) for definition. Opposite right: These distinctive, post-modernist cupboards by Charles Jencks have been sponged in a mid-brown (see page 127).

Above: A room of large proportions, this bedroom features enormous fitted cupboards either side of a dark gray-painted fireplace. Rather than try to disguise them, the artist has made a feature of them, by painting them white, dragging the panels (see page 128) and then lining them (see page 145) in a gray-blue. As a finishing touch, he has stencilled (see page 136) a classical urn filled with flowers, to fit neatly into the arching blue line.

𝒮MALL PIECES

Tilting mirrors for the dressing table, hair brushes and jewellery boxes all call for a delicate finish. Flowers and ribbons hand-painted or stencilled onto a plain background (see page 97) look beautiful on a small scale. And a tortoise-shell or lacquer finish would be exquisite.

Alternatively, try gilding very small items, such as cufflink or earring boxes, in a silver or gold finish. Such pieces will look especially effective when placed on a chest or dressing table that has been lacquered in a contrasting deep red or blue colour.

Above: The stencilled motifs (see page 136) adorning this collection of objects – plant pot, picture frame and lamp – were coloured in with stencil crayons. The stencils unify these otherwise disparate pieces, and their colours blend in very effectively with the peach, blue and yellow marbled desk.

CHILDREN'S ROOMS

Painting the furniture in a child's room is very enjoyable. Bold, vibrant colours can be used to create a stimulating atmosphere, and all manner of motifs can be liberally sprinkled around the room and over the furniture, to provide interest and encourage learning.

Above all, the decor of the room should have a sense of fun, be friendly and reflect the child's developing personality. The furniture can play a key role in achieving these ends and, quite simply, make the room an attractive place in which to work, rest and play.

ℬABIES' ROOMS

Of course, the character of a baby's room will be totally unlike that of a room designed for a school-age child or a teenager, as their requirements are quite different. Most parents prefer to use pastel shades, rather than bright primaries.

In a baby's room, the main piece of furniture will be a cot; and other items will probably include a playpen, a chest of drawers, a small table and a nursing chair. Try to give them a warm, friendly appearance by using sponged or ragged, soft pastel shades that complement the walls, carpet and curtains. And stencil a few furry animals or cartoon characters on top – particularly effective on the bars of the playpen. Make sure that you are using a safe paint – ideally choose a specially formulated nursery type.

Above: Using pretty pastel colours, this white Dragons' cot was decorated with friendly, cuddly characters. Floating balloons were added to the cot head, and the ribbons around the necks of the cuddly toys on the mobile were chosen to pick up the pastel colours on the cot. This understated style is very reassuring for a young child.

TODDLERS' ROOMS

As with a baby's room, the decor should not be over-stimulating – otherwise the toddler might become even more hyperactive. However, you can start to introduce a few notes of primary colour, to create a livelier atmosphere. Picking out drawer handles and matching them with the skirting board is but one option.

To encourage your child to learn, copy simple pictures of nursery characters from books – a toddler will have a particular favourite – and stencil them discreetly over some pieces, adding a stencilled alphabet and numbers close by.

This is the ideal time to include a *trompe l'oeil* mural on, for example, the front of a cupboard. Keep it simple and, if you're feeling adventurous, let the child help with the easier stages!

Above: Bright, stimulating colours were used to decorate the bed and shelves in this toddler's bedroom. The Winnie the Pooh motif hanging from dark blue balloons featured on the blind, was copied and traced onto the foot and head of the bed. And several other Pooh characters were transferred onto the shelving above the bed, in a lively dancing line – all standing out well against the contrasting white background.

CHILDREN'S ROOMS

Once a child starts school, his or her requirements begin to change. A desk will be needed for small amounts of homework, shelving required for books and a wardrobe necessary for hanging up school clothes. Together with desk lamps, mirrors, a proper bed and a toy chest, the quantity of furniture in the room will be steadily rising.

Consequently, it is all the more important to co-ordinate separate items within the scheme as a whole. If the furniture clashes with the decor it will make the room seem smaller, and a sense of space is very important to a growing child.

School-age children like writing their name on their possessions, so consider personalizing a piece of furniture – a chair, desk, crayon or toy box, for instance – with your child's name (see pages 88–91).

Whatever paint technique(s) you decide to use – and an older child is likely to appreciate more sophisticated effects such as stippling, dragging or lining – make sure you include the wastepaper basket as well as the wardrobe!

Above: You can tell a lot about the interests of the child who sleeps and plays in this bedroom by the painted themes he has chosen as decoration. The cricket board and players were painted directly onto the wall – there is no real blackboard here. And trompe l'oeil cartoon flying machines and their pilots provide the link between the bedhead and the chest of drawers, which was first dragged a deep coral colour (see page 128). Cars also feature on the chest, and a little mouse was painted at the bottom of the door – just for fun!

$\mathcal{T}$EENAGERS' ROOMS

Most teenagers spend a lot of time in their rooms – studying, listening to music and chatting to their friends – so it is important that they should enjoy their surroundings.

By now, the last thing they would want is to be taken for a child, especially by their peers. So, sit down and discuss the decorations with them. Depending on their personality and interests their taste in painted furniture will vary enormously. Some may want a pretty, romantic look, with sponged, soft pastel shades and stencilled floral displays on everything from the bedhead to the curtains, as here. While others will prefer geometric shapes and stronger colours, a black-and-gray high-tech look, or even elegant and sophisticated 'grown-up' finishes such as marbling, wood-graining and lacquering, with a complete absence of stencilled motifs altogether.

Again, whatever finish you or they decide to use on the furniture, make sure it complements the rest of the decor. Otherwise you will further diminish that ever-decreasing sense of space.

Above: This very romantic bedroom has a sophisticated air about it – which appeals greatly to the teenager to whom it belongs. The pink drapes hanging on the four-poster bed, and covering the kidney-shaped dressing table, accentuate the romantic flavour. Pink was also used as a motif colour for the stripped wooden chest at the foot of the bed – floral motifs, garlands and dancing ribbons being traced and painted on top. Smaller, more delicate flowers were painted on the dragged green table.

CRAYON BOX

I wanted to give a colourful, personalized present to a child, and asked an artist, Nessa Kearney, to decorate an old pencil box in a suitable style. The application of a coat of paint, the child's name and a favourite character, produced a remarkable transformation, and a wonderful present. The simplicity of the techniques used to achieve these impressive results would make this an ideal project for someone new to decorative painting.

1 *Nessa prepared the surface, applying a white eggshell ground (see page 118), and when dry, lining the edge of the box (see page 144).* **2** *Smudges were cleaned with rag and white spirit.* **3** *When the lining dried, Nessa applied a thin, light brown glaze and dragged a small decorators' brush through it to produce a wood-grained effect.* **4** *Letters were traced (from a*

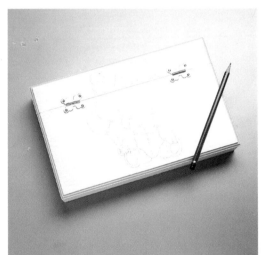

book), spacing them evenly. **5** *Nessa reversed the tracing paper, and ran over the outlines a number of times, with a soft lead pencil. Note: trace the outline of the teddy and balloons in the same way.* **6** *She turned the tracing paper over again, positioning it on the box and, pressing hard with a pencil, transferred the outlines onto the surface below.* **7** *The motifs are ready for colouring.* **8** *Covering the rest of the outline with paper, to avoid smudging, Nessa coloured in the letters.*

9

10

9 *Nessa gradually moved down the box,
always keeping the unpainted pencil outline
covered to avoid smudging, and filled in the
colours, using a different brush for each one.*
10 *She added details such as the teddy's
eyes, and applied shading and highlights to
the balloons and the teddy's paws and feet.*
11 *Finally, when the surface dried, she applied
one or two coats of clear polyurethane
varnish for protection.*

11

COTS AND BEDS

A cot can be made much more friendly to a child by painting or stencilling (see page 84) a line of cartoon characters, animals or balloons across the top bar. Moreover, provided lead-free paint is used, the framework can be painted to match the colour scheme in the rest of the room.

When the child graduates to a bed, a number of possibilities arise: standard bunks and beds with wooden headboards can be painted or stencilled with anything from teddies to superheroes or spattered with bright primary colours. Alternatively, if the frame of the bed is shaped in the basic outline of a racing car or a boat, for example, many details can be painted on freehand.

Top left: Black provides a good foil to the horse and rider painted in the top centre of this distinctive-looking bedhead. And the lettering on the stylized scroll identifies the owner of the bed. Top right: In complete contrast, the head of this white painted cot was decorated with a friendly, pastel-coloured bunny motif, taken from the quilt design. Bottom left: For an older child, the head of her bed was dragged in pastel green (see page 128), before adding a floral group, in greens, blues and pink, in the curve of the bedhead. The motif was continued onto the lampshade. Bottom right: Even more romantic is this fairytale bed. Ribbons and bows were stencilled in pink (see page 136) around the turned posts and on the head and foot of the bed. And the theme was continued on the adjacent wooden chest of drawers. Opposite right: This bed by Charles Jencks fits neatly against the wall and under the window, to make a very strong post-modernist form. The plain cream colour and the simple repeating design do not distract from the distinctive shape of the bed.

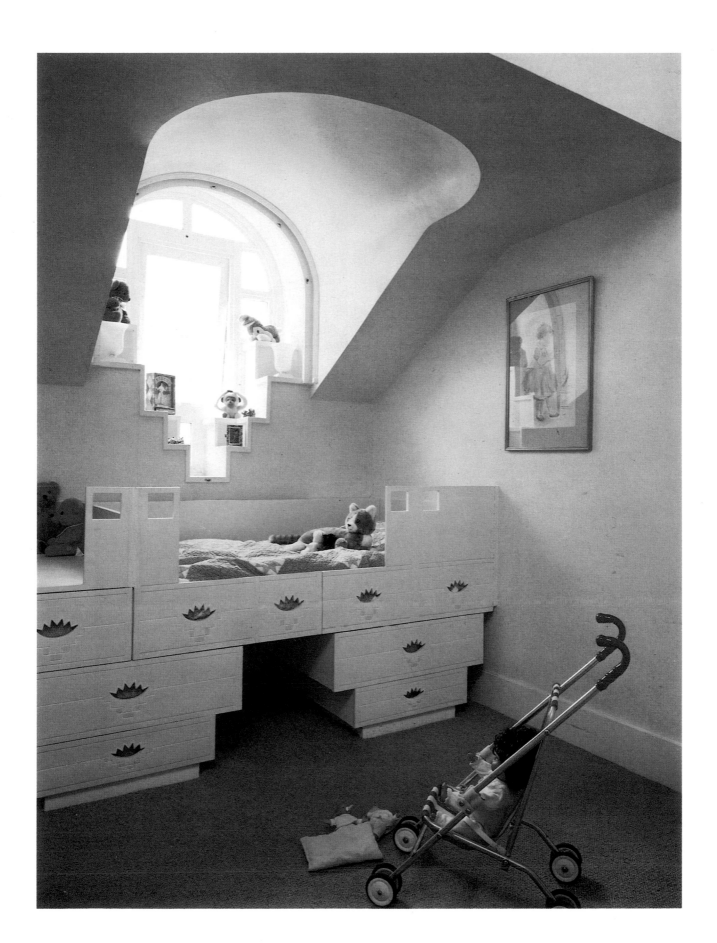

$\mathcal{S}$TORAGE FURNITURE

By the time a child has acquired enough clothes to fill a grown-up chest of drawers and wardrobe, he or she will probably have definite ideas as to how they should be decorated! However, before that stage arrives, try stippling, dragging or colourwashing bedroom furniture with the pre-dominant colour used elsewhere in the room, and then either painting or stencilling a motif of the child's favourite flower, animal or character onto the front of the drawers or doors. You could paint the motif onto the curtain fabric too, to tie the room scheme together.

As most children are very possessive about their toyboxes, it is a good idea to stencil the name of the owner and pictures of the contents, such as trains and cars, on to the top or side of the container. Again, the base colour should match the chest of drawers, bed and wardrobe, for a co-ordinated look.

Opposite left (top): This Victorian-style toy chest was decorated with stencilled motifs (see page 136), and coated with polyurethane varnish tinted with rust-coloured paint, to give it an antique finish. Opposite left (bottom): The fitted cupboard under the stairs was given a new lease of life by a trompe l'oeil *painting. Above: The strong green and blue floral design on the curtains in this bedroom provided the inspiration for the floral garlands and trail on the large desk, which was first dragged in cream (see page 128). To co-ordinate the various items in the room, the floral motif was also painted on the back of the chair, all around the wastepaper bin and on top of the pencil box.*

DESKS

It is a good idea to paint a child's desk in a bright, attractive colour (or their favourite one) to encourage them to sit at it. As with the storage furniture, paint (see page 89) the child's name on top of the desk or along a drawer front, to establish ownership. And add various stencilled or traced characters to provide a touch of fun and individuality.

Older children might appreciate a sponged, stippled, dragged or lined desk – but ask them first: they might want to try a spattered ink finish on their own!

Above: Gaby McCall stripped and sanded down this solid oak school desk, before rubbing white emulsion paint into the grain. Using crumpled kitchen paper, she wiped off some of the paint in places, to produce a mottled 'antique' finish. Then she stencilled motifs (see page 136) on the top, sides and legs of the desk.

SMALL PIECES

As with most of the furnishings in a child's room, when decorating smaller items you may want to try to strike a balance between simply making them look attractive and incorporating an 'educational' component.

Thus, small boxes and child-size chairs and tables can be painted with colours picked up from elsewhere in the room, such as the walls or curtains, and then motifs, letters and numbers hand-painted or stencilled on top, to assist the learning process. Similarly, the wooden surround of a wall clock might be painted in a suitable colour, and the numbers 1–12 hand-painted or stencilled in position around the rim, in a contrasting shade.

And wastepaper baskets can be decorated in bright colours, with the name of their young owner painted on the side, to encourage tidiness.

Above: The small items sitting on top of this kidney-shaped dressing table were painted in pastel colours. The swing mirror with the small drawer beneath, the small jewellery box and the brush were all stippled (see page 131) in pastel pink and decorated with floral motifs, to co-ordinate with the dressing table and curtain fabric.

BATHROOMS

All too often a bathroom is seen simply as a functional room – just somewhere to wash, shave and brush your teeth. Yet it should and can be much more than that. That is, a place where you can relax and unwind as well as wash. Painting the furniture and fixtures in a style sympathetic to the setting will help transform your bathroom into just such a retreat, whilst adding character and style to what is usually a rather featureless part of the home.

CHOOSING COLOURS

Nowadays most bathrooms are small, confined areas. And by painting fitted cupboards with broken colour techniques to harmonize with the walls, floor, curtains and towels, you will create a co-ordinated look that will increase the sense of space in the room.

Equally, in large bathrooms the inclusion of free-standing items such as cupboards or chairs, painted with colours or motifs used elsewhere in the room, will create a more intimate and appealing setting.

The colour(s) of your suite, tiles and major fittings will dictate the colours you choose to paint the furniture. For example, if white is your starting point you can suggest clean lines, efficiency and space by simply painting the furniture white as well. However, if you want to create a more relaxing atmosphere use complementary soft pastel colours and off-whites.

If, on the other hand, you are stuck with an old suite in a somewhat unfashionable colour, such as primrose yellow, don't despair. By painting cupboards in a soft gray or even primrose yellow itself, you will create a stylish look.

Above: Sizeable bathrooms, usually converted from bedrooms, give plenty of scope for furniture, but require a careful choice of colour scheme, as here, to unite all the otherwise disparate elements.

CHOOSING FINISHES

Any of the broken colour techniques outlined on pages 127–151 can be used to decorate furniture in the bathroom. The finish you choose will depend on what you are trying to achieve. For example, marbling, tortoiseshelling and wood-graining will create a rich, opulent effect most appropriate in luxury bathrooms. While sponging will produce a light, stylish look that will increase the sense of space and, depending on the colour used, evoke a subtle atmosphere – blues recalling the seaside and green the country, for example.

Stencilling is another technique that will allow you to pull all the features of the setting together, or if the room is en-suite with a bedroom, to co-ordinate the two. Simply embellish the suite and furniture with motifs taken from tiles and fabrics elsewhere in the room(s).

Finally, whatever colours or effects you choose, it is important that, given the presence of water, steam and condensation in a bathroom, you use oil- rather than water-based paints (see page 122). Eggshell is most effective, but even so most finishes will require additional coats of varnish to keep moisture at bay (see page 123).

Above: The brown and cream faux marbre on the sides of the bath and the stippled cream finish on the chest of drawers complement the rest of the colour scheme, and combine to give an air of faded grandeur to this sophisticated bathroom.

PROJECT FIVE

Co-ORDINATED BATHROOM

Inspired by the creative atmosphere of Charleston (see page 16), where she spent many summers as a child, Cressida Bell painted almost every surface in this bathroom with bold, brightly coloured shapes. After applying the background colour, she pencilled in the simple outlines, and then blocked in the contrasting colours one at a time. The naive style of the motifs make this an ideal project for the beginner to copy – a slightly uneven edge to a motif may even add to its charm!

1

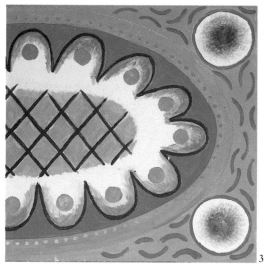

1 *Using blue and orange as her main colours, Cressida painted a stylized wave border and a fish onto the bath panels.* **2** *The wave border used around the bath was also set into the door panels.* **3** *This detail shows the bold, free style of Cressida's brushwork.* **4** *This small bookcase was painted in white emulsion, then decorated with a flower and pot design. Here, Cressida is seen dabbing on the large 'dots' of white glaze.* **5** *This chair has been decorated to co-ordinate with the bookcase – the grapes are framed with the same white 'dots' of glaze. The blue and white flourish on the central back rail serves as a foil to the strong blue lined verticals.*

6

6 & 7 *To protect her bold, decorative patterns – essential in a steamy bathroom – Cressida coated all the painted surfaces with two coats of clear polyurethane varnish (see page 123).*
Even though supposedly clashing colours are used throughout, they are combined to great effect – primarily, because Cressida's use of curving line and pattern is extended to all the painted surfaces, thereby harmonizing all the different colours and elements into a striking whole.

7

FITTED FURNITURE

bathrooms

Fitted furniture in the bathroom, such as vanity units and cupboards fitted above the basin or under the bath, can be painted to increase the sense of space in what is usually a small room. For example, if you have marbled, stencilled, spattered or sponged the floor or walls, continue the technique on the vanity unit and the sides of the bath, for an integrated look.

Alternatively, if you want a more decorative effect, you could apply a soft coloured wash to the cupboards, and then either hand-paint or stencil suitable seashore motifs, such as shells or starfish, on top.

Finally, remember that all surfaces in a bathroom will be subject to water, condensation and steam. So, either protect the finish with polyurethane varnish, or use an oil-based eggshell finish paint, rather than a water-based emulsion.

Above: There is an Art Nouveau feel to this bathroom, designed by Althea Wilson. A huge and languid-looking flower was painted on the tiles, below the light-blue-sponged wall, and another applied over the two doors of the unit under the washbasin. A good example showing that motifs do not have to be contained within panels or door frames to look effective. Opposite right: The panels of the bath and fitted linen cupboards were sponged (see page 127) and their surrounds dragged (see page 128), in a blue-green colour, before the 'Cornish Thrift' stencil (designed by Lyn le Grice) was applied (see page 136) in pink, green and ochre, to create a rustic look in this airy bathroom.

FREE-STANDING PIECES

Items such as chairs, stools and wooden towel rails can be painted using any number of broken colour techniques. But with space at a premium try to match them into the overall colour scheme, otherwise they may look too obtrusive and create a sense of clutter.

If you have a traditional, free-standing bathroom suite, a stencilled blue border of waves or shells around the rim of the bath, basin and even toilet looks very effective. The border could be applied to furniture too – along a chair back or round a linen bin, for example.

Above: The bright, busy floral wallpaper calls for a restrained use of colour on the washstand and chair. Consequently, they were colourwashed in green (see page 133), and embellished with discreet blue motifs. Opposite (top): The bath in this very grand bathroom was painted cream to match the wallpaper, and a simple stencilled border added along its sides. The chest of drawers was given a fantasy wood grain effect. Opposite (bottom): The towel rail was painted to look like bamboo (see page 140), and complement the pine floorboards with the stencilled shell border.

$\mathcal{H}$ALLS

Although a visitor gains his or her first impressions of a house from the entrance area, halls are often (mistakenly) overlooked as far as decorations and furniture are concerned. Despite their irregular shape, they should be considered as rooms in their own right, and attention should be given to the appearance of any furniture and how it fits in with the rest of the decor. An attractively furnished entrance hall can set the tone for the rest of the house.

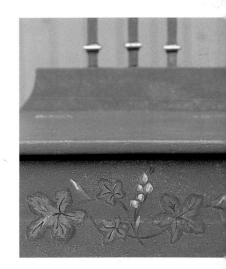

Furnishing Entrances

Even the smallest and narrowest of halls usually has space for a slim console table, hatstand or small chair. Provided such pieces are painted in a colour and style that co-ordinates with the walls, floor and any soft furnishings, they won't visually intrude into the limited sense of space. Indeed, they can add character and charm to what is often a rather stark and featureless area.

In large entrance halls, elegant furniture is virtually essential to establish an impression of tasteful grandeur. There is the space, and therefore the opportunity, to decorate free-standing pieces such as hallstands, cupboards, chests and dressers with some of the more elaborate paint techniques. You could experiment with effects like marbling or tortoiseshelling, which might look too striking or overpowering in a more confined setting.

But, whether your hall is large or small, modern or traditional, it is important that the furniture complements the surroundings. Thus, for example, by all means use the same stencils on the furniture as on the walls; or pick a motif from the wallpaper to decorate the hall table, chair or chest. However, don't get carried away and apply motifs everywhere, or what started out as a finishing touch could well end up as a blinding jumble of colours and shapes that will have the unwanted effect of dazzling, rather than welcoming, your guests.

Above left: An elegant, dark gray painted console table and a delicately curved chair stand out against a light gray ragged wall (see page 130). Both pieces relate to the huge door, which is also ragged in a dark gray. A colour scheme such as this requires a large space to avoid being slightly oppressive. Above right: Also employing two tones of the same colour, this grand hall has a lighter, more restful air. The French Empire stool was gilded, and relates both to the imposing portrait above, with its gilded frame, and to the gold-painted corrugated stand for the telephone. A good example of the way colour can unite seemingly disparate pieces. Opposite: This narrow but opulent hallway, with its rich, deep green door and wall and rich red curtain, demands an elegant piece of furniture. The intricately gilded console table with a white marble top fits the bill, and is in keeping with the gilded mirror frame above.

Small tables are often placed in an entrance hall to provide a surface for necessities such as the telephone, messages, the post, and a clock. Although such tables function as something of a workhorse, they are usually the first item of furniture that visitors to the home see.

If the decor is traditional, give your table an elegant finish by lacquering, gilding (see page 113), antiquing or wood-graining it to match the bannisters or coatstand. In a modern setting a dragged or ragged finish (see page 112) would be more appropriate. But bear in mind that halls are often dark, so it is a good idea to use a bright colour.

Small, free-standing storage cupboards should be viewed in the same light as hall tables; namely, that whilst they are functional they are often sited in a prominent position and should be decorated accordingly. Thus, lacquering, gilding (see page

112) and wood-graining are very effective in a traditional setting, whilst dragging is more suitable for a modern decor. Whereas in a country style entrance, stencilling the bare wood (usually pine) with rural motifs, such as birds or baskets of fruit, would be appropriate.

Coatstands can be spruced-up by painting or stencilling with garlands of flowers – this would be particularly effective in a Victorian-style setting (see page 110). For a modern interior a fantasy marble effect would be more appropriate.

Entrance areas are favourite places to hang mirrors or pictures (see pages 112–3), and their frames are perfect 'canvases' for paint effects like gilding or tortoiseshelling. Clocks, too, are often found in halls, and can be decorated in many ways. Try traditional stencilled or hand-painted floral motifs for a country home, wood-graining or marbling for a town house.

Above: An elegant, but rather dull wall clock was made more striking by painting it bright red. The golden colour of the eagle on top was picked up in the floral motifs along the bottom and down the centre panels. The motifs were traced onto the surface and the panels were then lined in gold (see page 144), to define the flowers and lend a more formal note. Opposite right: This white painted cupboard stands out against the dark blue wall, and illustrates the effectiveness of strongly contrasting colours.

$\mathcal{T}$ECHNIQUES

Paint finishes are a wonderful way to decorate furniture, but to guarantee the best results take time to get acquainted with your tools and materials, and be sure to follow my advice on the best way to prepare the surface you plan to paint.

PREPARING SURFACES

Before applying a decorative paint finish to any piece of furniture it is very important to prepare the surface correctly – whether it be wood, metal or melamine, painted or unpainted. However tempted you may be to do so, you must not skimp this stage of a project, as both the successful appearance and robustness of your painted finish will depend to a large extent on diligent preparation.

Sound painted surfaces

If the piece of furniture is already painted and the surface is in sound condition, with no sign of flaking or peeling paint, you can apply a new finish on top of the old one after carrying out a few simple preparations.
1 Wash the surface thoroughly with a warm solution of sugar soap, using a sponge or rag, to remove dust, grease and dirt. Particularly stubborn dirt or scuff marks can be shifted with a light scouring cream and an abrasive cloth. Then rinse thoroughly with clean water.
2 Rub down the surface with medium grade wet-and-dry abrasive paper (silicon carbide),

and rinse again with warm water. This will provide a key for the new coat of paint.
3 When dry, remove any dust with a soft brush and apply an oil-based undercoat followed by two coats of flat-oil or eggshell (both in the appropriate colour for the top coat).

Painted surfaces with minor damage

If the piece of furniture is painted, but has a few small areas of peeling, blistering or flaking paint, you will need to make some minor repairs before you begin applying a new paint finish.

1 Wash the entire surface thoroughly with a warm solution of sugar soap, to remove dust, dirt and grease, and rinse with clean water.
2 Using a spokeshave or stripping knife, scrape off the damaged section of paint.
3 Feather out the hard edges of the sound paint around the area that needs repair, using medium grade wet-and-dry paper (silicon carbide). Rinse, dry and seal with a thinned coat of PVA adhesive.
4 Apply a fine grade surface filler to the damaged area, to stand slightly proud of the surrounding paintwork. When dry, rub down with fine grade sandpaper.

Glazes can be applied on top of a sound painted eggshell surface, provided the surface was thoroughly cleaned, sanded and dusted before the eggshell coat was brushed on.

5 Rub down the entire surface with medium grade wet-and-dry paper (silicon carbide). Rinse with clean water.
6 When dry, remove any dust with a soft brush, and apply a coat of primer to the bare surface. Then apply an oil-based undercoat followed by two coats of flat-oil or eggshell (both in the appropriate colour for the top coat).

Melamine or laminate-faced chipboard

Old kitchen units are often faced with a melamine or plastic laminate finish. These surfaces must be keyed properly to accept a new coat of paint. Simply follow the method for preparing sound painted surfaces (see opposite). However, when you reach stage 2 it is very important to use a coarse grade of wet-and-dry paper (silicon carbide), rather than a medium grade.

Painted surfaces with major damage

Any painted surface which is suffering from extensive blistering, peeling or flaking must be stripped back to the bare wood (or metal). This can be done either with a chemical paint stripper or a blow lamp or hot air stripper. Whilst chemical stripping is more expensive, there is little or no danger of damaging the wood underneath, as there is with a blow torch. So, whilst both techniques are outlined here, the second is recommended.

Burning off

1 Open the window to allow unpleasant fumes to escape, and put on thick, cotton gardening gloves and rubber goggles, to protect your hands and eyes. Stand the piece of furniture on aluminium cooking foil, to protect the floor from flakes of burning paint.
2 Play the heat from the blow torch or electric stripper over the surface, and as the paint begins to bubble scrape it off with a stripping knife. Wood will char and blacken very easily, so don't concentrate the heat on any one area for too long.
3 You will need to remove the paint from any mouldings with a chemical stripper and grade 0 wire wool. Rub in the direction of the grain.
4 Finally, rub down the entire surface with white spirit and grade 000 wire wool, and repeat using a soft, lint-free rag. Then follow the instructions for preparing bare wood (see page 120).

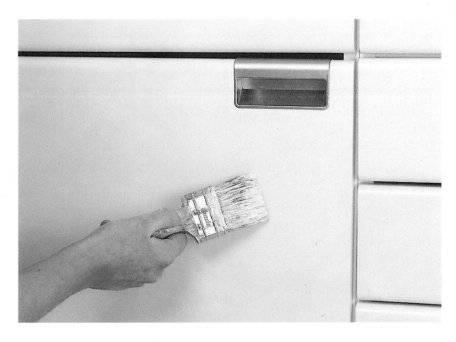

Melamine or laminate surfaces can be painted as long as they are thoroughly prepared (see above). Effective sanding is most important.

Chemical stripping

1 Open the windows to allow unpleasant fumes to escape, and put on industrial strength rubber gloves and plastic goggles, to protect your hands and eyes.

2 Brush on a coat of spirit-based chemical stripper (don't use water-based stripper as it may raise the grain of the wood or encourage rust if the underlying surface is metal), and leave for 30 minutes. Then brush on a second coat.

3 As the layers of paint begin to soften and wrinkle strip them away, using a shave hook, stripping knife, grade 0 wire wool and an old toothbrush on any intricate areas such as mouldings. Apply further coats of chemical stripper, as necessary.

4 When all the paint has been removed, clean the surface thoroughly with liberal quantities of white spirit, using a soft rag or sponge. This will neutralize any remnants of the stripper. Then follow the instructions for preparing bare wood (see below).

Bare wooden surfaces

If a bare wooden surface, having been stripped of its painted, waxed or varnished finish, reveals any gashes or unsightly nail holes these will need to be repaired before a new finish can be applied.

1 Apply two coats of metal primer to any exposed nail or screw heads evident just below the surface.

2 Fill any gaps or holes with a flexible wood filler, pressing it firmly home with a knife. (Some fillers require you to apply a primer coat to the bare wood first – follow the instructions on the tin.) Level off with the surrounding surface, and allow to dry for at least 24 hours.

3 The filler will contract as it dries, so apply a coat of fine grade filler on top, to stand proud of the surrounding surface. When dry, rub it down with fine grade sandpaper to produce a flat, smooth finish.

4 If the earlier stripping process has raised the grain of the wood, rub it down with progressively fine grades of sandpaper.

5 If removal of the old finish has exposed any knots, these must be coated with two coats of (white) knotting compound. Allow to dry between coats.

6 Apply a coat of oil-based wood primer to the entire surface and allow to dry. Now apply an oil-based undercoat, followed by two coats of flat-

It is very important to prepare bare wood thoroughly before painting (see above). Poor preparation will adversely affect your result.

oil or eggshell, rubbing down with a fine grade sandpaper between coats.

Waxed and oiled surfaces

Wax-polished and oiled finishes will not take a painted finish, and therefore must be removed. Simply apply white spirit to the surface, using a lint-free rag or grade 000 wire wool. Rub in the direction of the grain. The old finish will gradually dissolve. Then follow the instructions for preparing bare wood (see page 120).

Varnished or shellacked surfaces

Varnished surfaces in good condition can be cleaned, rubbed down with fine grade sandpaper, rinsed and dried prior to redecorating. However, it is preferable if the varnish is removed.

Shellac finish Remove shellac with methylated spirit and 00 grade wire wool. Then follow the instructions for preparing bare wood (see page 120).

Cellulose finish Remove a cellulose-based lacquer or varnish with spirit-based liquid paint stripper (see page 120) or a proprietary hard finish remover. Then follow the instructions for preparing bare wood (see page 120).

Metal surfaces

Previously painted metal in sound condition should be prepared following the method outlined for sound painted surfaces (see page 118). However, a painted finish in unsound condition, showing flaking, peeling or blistered paint and evidence of rust, must be removed.

1 Open the window to allow unpleasant fumes to escape. Put on rubber gloves and goggles to protect hands and eyes. Brush on several coats of a spirit-based chemical stripper to loosen the layers of paint.
2 As the paint begins to blister, scrape it off with grade 1 wire wool and/or a wire brush.
3 Clean the bare metal with white spirit and a lint-free rag.
4 If there is evidence of rusting, apply two coats of a rust inhibitor, followed by a coat of metal primer.
5 Apply an oil-based undercoat followed by two coats of flat-oil or eggshell, rubbing down between coats. (Use undercoat and eggshell in an appropriate colour for the top coat.)

Scour, prime, and apply undercoat and eggshell before applying a glaze to a metal surface. As with carved wood, work well into any mouldings.

PAINT, GLAZES AND VARNISHES

Before looking at the various paints and glazes available for decorating furniture, it is worth noting that in addition to the leading paint companies' comprehensive range of products, artists' suppliers will provide custom colours, glazes and specialist brushes.
But wherever you buy your paint and materials, always choose the best quality you can afford, and for the best results be sure to follow the manufacturer's instructions relating to matters such as drying times, appropriate solvents and undercoats.

Water-based paints and glazes

Emulsions are available in matt, silk and gloss finishes, and come in a wide range of colours. Unfortunately they have three main shortcomings as far as the application of broken colour techniques to furniture is concerned. Firstly, their fast drying times restrict the time available for working the wet paint to produce the required effect. Secondly, being water-based they can raise the grain when applied to bare wood and induce rust on bare metal. And thirdly, they produce a finish that is unsuitable for sanding, making it difficult to achieve a smooth finish if they are used as a top coat, which is particularly important when lacquering (see page 146) or marbling (see page 150), for example.

Consequently, for both ground and top coats you are advised to use oil-based paints. However, an exception is when colourwashing (see page 133): a matt or mid-sheen emulsion glaze or wash can be prepared by thinning it with as many as eight parts water, to produce a soft, subtle finish when applied to woods such as pine.

Rather than buying ready-coloured retail paint for colourwashing effects, you can mix your own by adding artists' gouache colours (available from artists' suppliers) to white emulsion. Although more expensive, this will provide a superior finish.

Artists' acrylics

Although a polymer binder is used to support the pigment, like emulsions acrylics are thinned with water, and therefore as a glaze or wash they have all the attendant disadvantages as far as decorating furniture is concerned (see 'Water-based paints and glazes'). However, their very fast drying time makes them useful for stencilling (see page 136) and producing swift overlays of colour in techniques such as ragging (see page 130).

Oil-based paints

An ideal medium for decorating furniture, oil-based paints come in a number of formulations.

Primers are used on bare wood and metal to prepare the surface for the ground coat.

Undercoats are used on top of primers and previously painted surfaces. They provide a non-porous background for flat-oil and eggshell finish ground coats, and help to fill minor imperfections in the surface. If the required shade is unavailable, colours can be made up by tinting white undercoat with artists' oils (see 'Mixing and tinting glazes').

Flat-oil paint is used on top of an undercoat to provide a high quality, matt finish ground coat for a decorative top coat(s). It is only available from specialist suppliers. As with undercoat, colours can be made up by adding artists' oils to a white base (see 'Mixing and tinting glazes').

Eggshell paint provides a soft, mid-sheen finish, and can be used both as a ground coat for a decorative top coat, and as the finish or top coat itself. Custom colours can be made up by adding artists' pigment to a white base, and glazes and washes can be produced by thinning with up to eight parts white spirit (see 'Mixing and tinting glazes').

Gloss paint, as its name implies, provides a shiny finish or top coat. However, it is rarely used when applying a broken colour technique to furniture. If a highly reflective finish is required, as in certain types of lacquering (see page 146), a gloss varnish is used as a top coat instead.

Oil-based glazes

These glazes are the traditional media for broken colour techniques.

Scumble glaze is an oil-based liquid (available from artists' suppliers) which becomes colourless when thinned in a ratio of 1 part scumble to 1 or 2 parts white spirit, depending on the consistency required. It is tinted to the required colour using artists' oils, and provides a high quality finish with a degree of transparency in the colour, which is particularly important to such techniques as dragging (see page 128), tortoiseshelling (see page 138) and marbling (see page 150).

Thinned paint glaze is undercoat or eggshell paint thinned with white spirit to achieve the required transparency of colour. However, it dries quicker than scumble glaze, and therefore can be more difficult to work – though adding one teaspoon of boiled linseed oil to half a litre of glaze will lengthen the drying time. Artists' oils can be added to produce the required colour.

Oil-based washes are made by thinning tinted, oil-based paint with up to 8 parts white spirit. Like water-based washes, they reveal just a subtle trace of colour when applied to a surface.

Artists' oils are available from artists' suppliers in a wide range of colours. They are used to tint white undercoat and eggshell paint as well as scumble glaze. Mixed with white spirit they produce vibrant coloured glazes and washes in their own right, but you should add one teaspoon of white undercoat to every litre of glaze to provide 'body', and thereby stop the glaze running down vertical surfaces.

Mixing and tinting glazes
When tinting oil-based glazes and washes it is important to create a uniform colouring throughout the mix. To be sure of this use either of the following methods:
1 Put a level teaspoon of artists' oil into a clean container, and add a similar quantity of white spirit. Mix them thoroughly to create a uniformly creamy consistency.
2 Add a small quantity of scumble glaze to the mix, and again blend thoroughly.
3 Slowly add this mixture to the rest of the scumble glaze, stirring all the time, until you have achieved the colour you require.
4 The mixture can then be thinned in a ratio of up to 1 part scumble glaze to 1 or 2 parts white spirit, until you have achieved the desired degree of transparency. If you require greater opacity in the glaze, try adding a little white eggshell to the mix.

Alternatively, if you are preparing a glaze from undercoat or eggshell paint:
1 Place sufficient paint for the job in a clean container.
2 Mix the artists' pigment with a similar quantity of white spirit and slowly blend it into the paint, until you have created the right colour.
3 Then add white spirit in sufficient quantity to create the desired transparency – a ratio of 1 part paint to 2 parts solvent is usually appropriate, but this can vary, depending on the degree of opacity that you require.

Finally, adopt a systematic approach to the preparation of paints and glazes. Follow the stipulated proportions, where indicated in the text, when mixing glazes for the various

broken colour techniques. However, do experiment: create 'samples' of different mixes on spare pieces of paper, and keep a note of the quantities used so you can, if needs be, replicate them at a future date.

Swedish-style glaze
This glaze produces an attractive matt finish.
1 In a glass jar, mix one egg, linseed oil equal to one egg, and double their volume of water. Whisk together.
2 In a second jar put a small quantity of artists' oil paint in your chosen colour, then pour in the first mix slowly until the glaze has the consistency of pancake batter.

Varnishes and spirit
As well as your paint or glaze, a supply of these products is needed.

Polyurethane varnishes come in matt, mid-sheen and gloss finishes, and provide a necessary protective coating for many paint finishes.

Goldsize is a quick-drying varnish used as an adhesive for gold or metal leaf (see gilding, page 152).

White spirit is used as a solvent and thinning agent for the creation of oil-based washes and glazes. It is also used for cleaning brushes, sponges and rags.

Equipment

A wide variety of equipment is available for paint techniques. Some items are sold in regular stores, but for certain tools, such as softening and stippling brushes, you will have to contact a specialist supplier. Don't rush out and buy all the equipment you might need at once, it is more economic to build up a collection slowly.

Paint tray

Polyurethane varnish

Metal saucer

China bowls

Steel combs

Beeswax polish

Lint-free rag

Scumble glaze

Artists' acrylics

Cotton buds

Metal powder

Stencilling brushes

Varnishing brush

Standard decorators' brushes

Artists' oils

PURE BRISTLES STAINLESS

PURE BRISTLES STAINLESS

WN Artists' Oil Colour Winsor Green 170SL Series 2

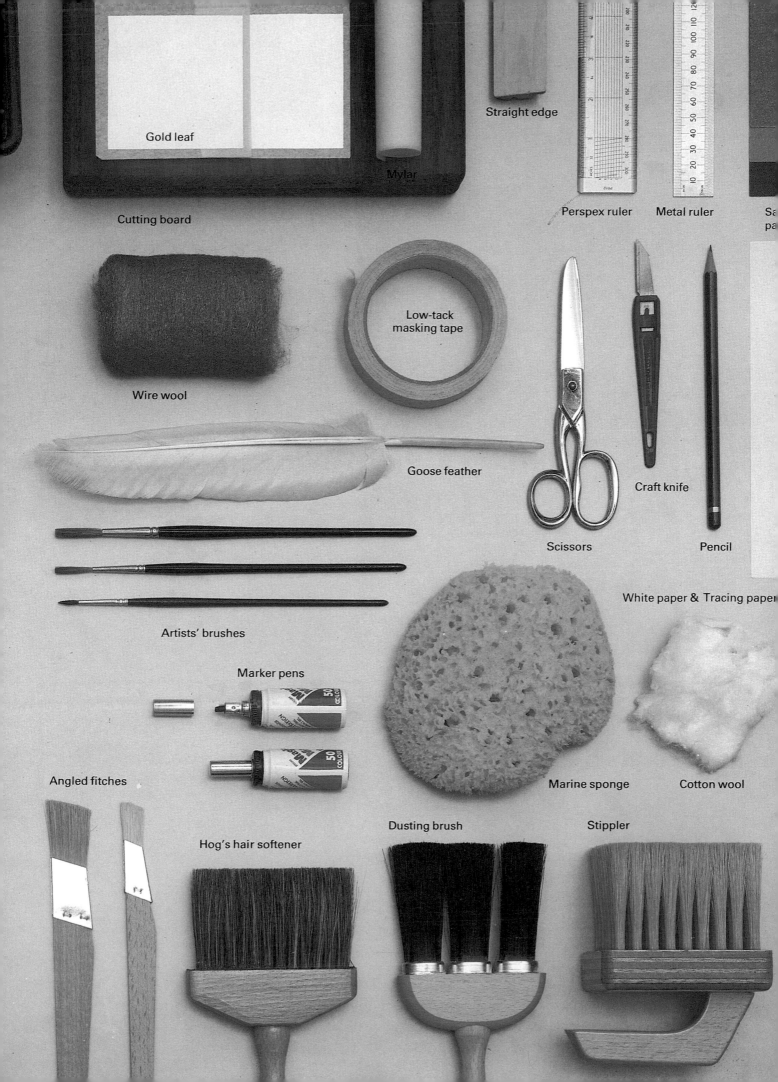

Gold leaf

Straight edge

Mylar

Perspex ruler

Metal ruler

Sa...
pa...

Cutting board

Wire wool

Low-tack
masking tape

Scissors

Craft knife

Pencil

Goose feather

Artists' brushes

White paper & Tracing paper

Marker pens

Marine sponge

Cotton wool

Angled fitches

Dusting brush

Stippler

Hog's hair softener

Standard decorators' brushes Available in 76 mm (3 in), 55 mm (2 in) and 25 mm (1 in) sizes. Used for the application of undercoats and ground coats as well as top coats. As with paint, buy the best you can afford, preferably pure bristle, as cheap brushes can spoil a finish.

Fitch An angled 12 mm (½ in) brush useful for working paints and glazes into angled recesses and mouldings.

Dust brush A soft-bristled brush used to remove dry dust from surfaces prior to painting.

Hog's hair softening brush An indispensable, if expensive, item of equipment. Used to soften and blend colours together in several paint techniques – notably marbling (see page 150) and wood-graining (see page 142). After use it should always be cleaned with white spirit, washed in soapy water and hung up to dry. A badger softener is a more pricey but superior alternative.

Stippling brush A hard-bristled brush used for stippling a glaze (see page 131).

Varnish brushes Buy in 76 mm (3 in), 55 mm (2 in), 25 mm (1 in) and 12 mm (½ in) sizes. They have more bristles to the square inch than standard decorators' brushes, and thus produce a 'cleaner', mark-free finish – though standard decorators' brushes are acceptable, and cheaper, alternatives.

Stencilling brush Short and stubby, this brush is designed for dabbing paint onto surfaces through the stencils.

Artists' brushes These are essential for painting fine details in a number of techniques. Sizes No. 3 and 6 are the most useful. Again, buy the best

quality you can afford.

Marine sponge Used for sponging (see page 127) and creating mottled effects on glazes in other techniques. Buy a sponge no larger than the size of your fist, otherwise it will be unmanageable. And for detailed work use thumb-sized pieces. Don't use synthetic sponges as they will produce too regular a print (unless this is the effect you require).

Rags Made from either chamois leather or lint-free cotton, they are used for ragging and rag-rolling (see page 130), as well as for rubbing over colours to soften their appearance.

Combs These can be made from cardboard if proprietary metal combs are unavailable. Use for displacing glaze in techniques such as marbling (see page 150).

Goose feather A tool for creating veins when marbling (see page 150).

Ceramic bowls For mixing and storing paints and glazes.

Palette and dippers Used for mixing small quantities of paint when producing detailed work.

Paint tray Useful for storing the glaze when sponging (see page 127).

Sandpaper Available in fine, medium and coarse grades. Used for rubbing down bare wooden surfaces prior to painting.

Wet-and-dry paper Also known as silicon carbide paper. Available in fine, medium and coarse grades. Used for keying previously painted surfaces prior to repainting, and for rubbing down between coats. Used wet, it will not create any dust.

Wire wool Available in grades 3 to 000 (the latter is the finest). More flexible than wet-and-dry

paper, and therefore more useful for rubbing down and keying curved or moulded painted surfaces.

Chemical paint stripper Liquid or paste for removing layers of paint and varnish. Spirit-based, rather than water-based, strippers are preferable, as they will not raise the grain of the underlying wood or induce metal to rust. Always use protective goggles and gloves, and open windows to allow unpleasant fumes to escape.

Gas and electric paint strippers These can be used instead of chemical strippers, but the danger of charring or burning the wood makes them an inferior option.

Spokeshaves and stripping knives Used in conjunction with paint strippers for scraping off unsound paint.

Flexible wood fillers Used for repairing damaged surfaces. They can also be mixed up into a very thin paste (spackle) to fill very open-grained woods.

Low-tack masking tape Useful both for securing stencils in position without damaging previously painted surfaces (see page 136), and for masking-off and protecting adjacent areas from paint when adding fine details.

Scissors and a sharp craft knife For cutting stencils (see page 134).

Clean rags For cleaning brushes and mopping up paint spills.

Plastic goggles and rubber gloves For protecting eyes and hands. Particularly important when using chemical paint strippers.

Mylar A transparent material for tracing and cutting-out stencils (available from artists' or specialist stencil suppliers).

$\mathscr{S}$PONGING

Sponging is a simple technique which produces a cloudy speckled finish that softens the features and outlines of furniture. This characteristic makes it a very effective method of toning down the visual presence of large, crude pieces such as old wardrobes and chests of drawers, especially if pastel colours are used. Whilst being a finish in its own right, sponging also can be used as a background for other effects such as lining (see page 144) and stencilling (see pages 134–7). Use a marine sponge when applying the glaze. This will produce a random pattern over the surface; whereas a synthetic sponge will produce a somewhat contrived uniform finish. Finally, build up the finish in stages: either by superimposing a darker tone of the original glaze on top of the first coat, or by sponging a different colour altogether on top.

1

2

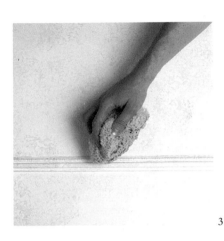

3

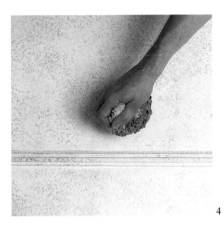

4

5

1 Mix up an oil-based glaze in the colour of your choice (see page 123) and pour it into a flat paint tray. Dip a marine sponge, previously soaked in white spirit and then wrung out, into the glaze. Don't overload it, and remove any excess glaze by dabbing the sponge on the side of the container. Then test both the colour and the print on a piece of spare paper.

2 Using a clean rag, wipe a thin layer of scumble glaze, diluted with a little white spirit, over a previously prepared flat-oil or eggshell ground (see pages 118–21).

3 Apply the glaze prepared in step 1, by gently dabbing the sponge over the wet scumble-glazed surface, leaving random gaps and spaces. Keep changing the position of the sponge in your hand, and recharge it with glaze when necessary. Test the print each time on clean paper, and clean the sponge regularly with white spirit to stop it becoming clogged with glaze – failure to do this will result in a smudged finish.

4 Either add more pigment to the original glaze, or mix up a new batch in a different colour and, using the same technique as in step 3, sponge on top of the completed first coat and fill in the gaps. If the first glaze has been allowed to dry you will achieve a sharper contrast between the two shades or colours; whereas if it is still wet, the finish will be softer and more blurred.

5 When the glazes have dried, apply one or two coats of clear matt or mid-sheen polyurethane varnish for protection, rubbing down with grade 000 wire wool between coats.

DRAGGING

Dragging is a simple technique that involves pulling either a specialist dragging brush or a hog's hair softener across a wet surface, to displace fine stripes of glaze and reveal a contrasting or complementary ground underneath. Used extensively in wood-graining (see page 142) to mimic the grain of wood, dragging produces regular patterned finishes of great subtlety and sophistication. When employed with natural wood colours or soft pastels it will lend an elegance to otherwise boring or featureless pieces of furniture, especially if you drag all vertical framework and panelled sections vertically, and all crosspieces horizontally.

1 Mix up a thinned eggshell or scumble glaze, tinted with artists' oil in the colour of your choice (see pages 122–3). Do not overthin the glaze, or it will dry too quickly on the surface.

2 Having made sure that the surface to be decorated is smooth (see pages 118–21) – as any bumps or hollows will interfere with the fine stripes produced by the dragging brush – apply a thin film of the glaze over the previously prepared flat-oil or eggshell ground coat (see pages 118–21).

3 Just before the glaze starts to become tacky, pull the hog's hair softener or dragging brush across the surface in a straight line, and in a continuous stroke, from one edge of the piece to the other. Use the sides, rather than the tip of the bristles.

4 At the end of each stroke wipe off the build-up of glaze on the brush on to a clean rag. Every so often you may need to clean the brush in white spirit, and then dry it thoroughly before recommencing.

5 When you have dragged the entire surface, allow the glaze to dry and then apply two coats of matt or mid-sheen clear polyurethane varnish for protection.

6 An optional step (prior to varnishing) is to create an abstract, two-directional look by repeating the dragging process in the opposite direction once the first coat has dried. You can use either a complementary or a contrasting glaze, but choose carefully, as certain colour combinations can give an overpowering result.

COMBING

Combing is a technique which employs an almost identical method to dragging. As the name implies, it involves pulling the teeth of a comb through a wet glaze to reveal fine stripes of the complementary or contrasting ground coat. You can buy special combs from artists' or decorators' suppliers, or make your own from pieces of rigid plastic or card. Homemade types have the advantage that you can determine the width both of the teeth and the gaps between them. Unlike dragging, the subtle contrasts between the different coloured glazes and ground coats tend to be less noticeable than the patterns produced. For this reason the technique is best restricted to smaller items.

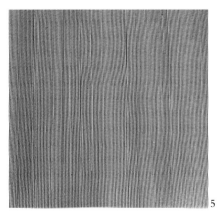

1 Mix up a thinned eggshell or scumble glaze, tinted with artists' oil in the colour of your choice (see page 123). Do not overthin the glaze, or it will dry too quickly on the surface.
2 Having made sure that the surface to be decorated is smooth (see pages 118–21) – as any bumps or hollows will interfere with the fine stripes produced by the comb – apply a thin film of the glaze over the previously prepared flat-oil or eggshell ground coat (see pages 118–21).

3 Just before the glaze becomes tacky, pull the comb across the surface in a straight line, and in a continuous movement, from one edge of the piece to the other.
4 At the end of each sweep wipe off the build-up of glaze on and between the teeth of the comb on to a clean rag. It may help to moisten the rag with a little white spirit.

5 When you have combed the entire surface, allow the glaze to dry and then apply two coats of matt or mid-sheen clear polyurethane varnish for protection.
6 An optional step (prior to varnishing) is to create an attractive mottled finish by pulling the comb through the still wet glaze over the top of the original lines, and at an angle of approximately 30 degrees to them, occasionally introducing a slight wiggle or waver into the sweep of the comb.

RAGGING AND RAG ROLLING

Ragging involves applying a coloured glaze to a surface, using a bunched-up rag made from virtually any lint-free material. The appearance of the resulting print depends on the type of material used and the way in which it is moved over the surface. For example, cheesecloth leaves an impression of soft wool and hessian produces a distressed leather finish. In all cases the result is quite dramatic, and for this reason muted pastel colours produce the best effects – more vibrant colours tend to be overpowering.
Rag-rolling is a variation of ragging, and involves bunching a rag into a sausage shape and rolling it over a surface to produce cloudy, almost marble-like effects.

1

2

3

4

5

6

1 Mix up an oil-based glaze in the colour of your choice (see page 123), and pour it into a flat paint tray. A thinned eggshell glaze will give a softer finish than a tinted scumble glaze.

2 If you are ragging: bunch the rag into a loose ball, dip it into the glaze and remove any excess on the side of the container and a spare piece of paper.

Apply the glaze to a previously prepared flat-oil eggshell ground coat with a dabbing and rocking action, continually varying the pressure and re-bunching the cloth.

This will stop the print becoming too regular, and allow the ground coat to ghost through in places. From time to time, either clean the rag with white spirit to stop it drying out and becoming clogged with glaze, or swop it for a new one.

3 When you have covered the entire surface allow the glaze to dry. Then, for a subtle two-tone effect, rag a complementary or contrasting coloured glaze over the top of the first one (this is optional).

4 Allow the glazes to dry and then apply two coats of matt or mid-sheen clear polyurethane varnish for protection.

5 If you are rag-rolling: bunch the rag into a sausage shape and roll it over the surface – again varying the direction and pressure to allow the ground coat to show through at random. Remember to clean or exchange the rag at regular intervals.

6 As with ragging, allow the glaze to dry before applying two coats of matt or mid-sheen polyurethane varnish for protection.

STIPPLING

Stippling is a simple technique which involves dabbing a flat-faced brush over a still wet glaze in order to remove small quantities of that glaze, and thereby reveal tiny pinpricks of the underlying ground in a contrasting colour. Ideally you should use a stippling brush, but as they are expensive, an old hairbrush or even dimpled kitchen paper are acceptable substitutes – the latter produces a soft, cloudy effect I call 'Dragon's stipple'. For the most effective results, the underlying ground coat should be a lighter colour than the transparent coloured glaze on top. Subtle shaded effects and gradations of colour can be produced by merging and blending sections of different toned or coloured glazes into each other, and feathering out the adjoining edges using the stippling brush.

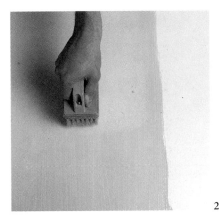

1 Mix up an eggshell or scumble glaze in the colour of your choice (see page 123), and, using a standard decorators' brush, apply a thin film of it over a previously prepared eggshell ground (see pages 118-21). If you are stippling over a large area, work in sections as the glaze dries quite rapidly.
2 Whilst the glaze is still wet, stipple the surface with the end of a stippling brush that has been slightly moistened with a little glaze. Use a firm and rapid dabbing action, but don't press too hard, or you may skid over the surface. Clean the brush at regular intervals on a rag soaked in white spirit, to avoid smudging the finish.
3 When you have finished the first section start on the next immediately. Try to keep a wet edge going to achieve a consistent finish and avoid obvious joins between the sections. Soften and blend the different sections together using the stippling action.

4 If there has been too great a build-up of glaze over some areas, this can be toned down by gently stippling with a brush moistened with a little white spirit. But be careful not to smudge the finish.
5 If you discover you have removed too much glaze from some areas, simply brush a thin film of glaze on to the bristles of the stippling brush and dab this over the appropriate patch, blending it into the surrounding area.
6 Finally, when the glaze has dried apply two coats of matt or mid-sheen clear polyurethane varnish for protection.

131

SPATTERING

Spattering is a simple technique which involves loading a stiff-bristled brush with glaze, holding it over the surface to be decorated, and then either tapping the handle of the brush or dragging a finger over the bristles, to spatter tiny droplets of the glaze over a contrasting ground coat. Additional glazes can be superimposed on top to build up delicate, speckled, multi-coloured finishes with a hint of texture. The size and pattern of the spattered droplets will depend on how hard you tap the brush or rake the bristles, and how far the brush is away from the surface. Consequently, in order to be able to control the effect, you are advised to practise first on a spare piece of paper.

1

2

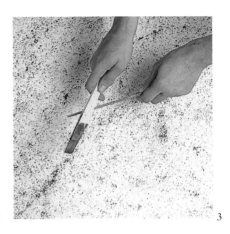
3

4

5

1 Mix up three thinned eggshell or scumble glazes (you can use less or more mixes if desired), tinted in the colours of your choice. The correct proportions for spattering are approximately 1 part glaze to 2 or 3 parts white spirit (or water, if you are using emulsions or artists' acrylics — see page 122).
2 Charge an angled fitch with the first glaze (don't overload it), and hold it some 10 or 12 cm (4 or 5 in) over a previously prepared flat-oil or eggshell ground (see pages 118–21).

Tap the handle of the fitch with another fitch (or a ruler) to spatter droplets of glaze over the surface — vary the strength of tapping and the distance of the fitch from the surface in order to adjust the size of the droplets. But be warned, large droplets can run, and will need to be blotted up quickly with some clean lint-free rag.

3 When the first glaze has dried, repeat the technique with the second glaze, gradually covering more and more of the ground coat.
4 Finally, charge a fitch with the darkest glaze (black mixed with a little burnt umber was used here), and drag your finger through the fitch bristles to send a very fine spray of droplets over patches of the surface.
5 When the final glaze has dried, apply two coats of matt or mid-sheen clear polyurethane varnish to the finished surface for protection.

Colourwashing

A colour wash is a coat of highly thinned transparent paint or glaze brushed over a white or pale-coloured ground to produce a soft, delicate, translucent coloured finish. To preserve its flattish quality colourwashing should be protected with a matt polyurethane varnish – never use a mid-sheen or gloss type.
The technique can be applied with either oil- or water-based paints (see page 122), though the latter will provide a softer finish. Colourwashing looks most effective when increasingly darker shades of the same colour are washed on top of each other. A soft, colourwashed effect is a particularly appropriate way to decorate simple, country-style pine furniture.

1

2

3

4

5

1 Prepare the surface of the piece of furniture and apply a white or pale-coloured matt or eggshell ground (see pages118–21). Allow to dry, then stand the piece on polythene sheeting to protect the surrounding area – colourwashing can be messy!
2 Prepare the wash in one of two ways. Either mix a flat oil-based coloured glaze, in the colour of your choice (see page 123), and dilute it to a wash using 1 part glaze to 8 or 9 parts white spirit; or dilute a tinted matt emulsion glaze (see pages 122–3), using 1 part paint to 8 or 9 parts water.

3 Using a large standard decorators' brush (7.5 cm/3 in on something the size of a wardrobe or kitchen table), apply the wash to the surface with an irregular, loose, slapping movement. Brush in all directions to stop the wash running off the surface (although some of it is bound to, especially with an emulsion wash). When you have covered the entire surface, allow the glaze to dry.

4 Don't worry if the first coat looks awful – it probably will. The application of a second and third wash will make all the difference. Build up as many coats as you like, until the required depth and transparency of colour is achieved, but allow to dry between coats.
5 Finally, colourwashing looks best as an unvarnished, natural matt finish. However, to be realistic some protection will be required with items such as pine kitchen tables, so apply two or three coats of matt finish clear polyurethane varnish.

STENCIL CUTTING

Stencilling is a technique which allows you to embellish the surface of almost any item of furniture with either simple or sophisticated pictures and motifs. Yet it demands none of the skills required by freehand painting. Stencil patterns are available commercially from artists' suppliers, and come in a variety of forms, including baskets and garlands of flowers; pieces of fruit; simple geometrics; numbers and letters; and cartoon characters.

1

2

3

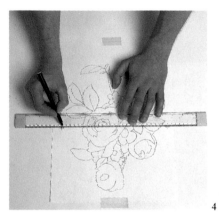

4

5

6

Copying the motif:

1 Drape the curtain over a flat surface and, using low-tack masking tape, position a sheet of tracing paper (available from artists' suppliers) over the pattern. Then, with a soft lead pencil, trace the outlines of the pattern onto the paper.
2 Remove the curtain, turn the sheet of tracing paper upside down, and go over the reverse of the pattern a number of times with the soft lead pencil.

3 Turn the tracing paper over again, and tape it in position on top of a sheet of paper. Press firmly over the outline a number of times with a pencil, to transfer the pattern to the paper below.
Then remove the tracing paper and put the paper through a photocopier with an enlarging or reducing facility (available in most high street copying shops) to increase or reduce the pattern to the required size.
4 Tape the photocopied pattern on to the flat surface and, using a pencil and ruler, make two registration crosses on either side of the paper.

5 Tape a sheet of clear 100 microns thick Mylar (available from artists' suppliers, and superior to the traditional card stencil material) on top of the pattern. Using a fine felt-tip pen, trace both the registration marks and the outlines of the leaves onto the Mylar.
6 Remove the Mylar, and tape a second sheet in place over the pattern. Again using a fine felt-tip pen, trace the two registration marks and the outlines of the smaller flowers.

However, you don't have to buy a stencil as it is easy to copy and cut out your own stencils; which means that you can decorate furniture with patterns and motifs found on other fixtures and furnishings in the room. For example, if you have either flowers or geometric shapes on your bedroom curtains, you can copy and 'repeat' them on the bedhead or the wardrobe. This will help to create a co-ordinated look, as well as adding interest and character.

7

9A

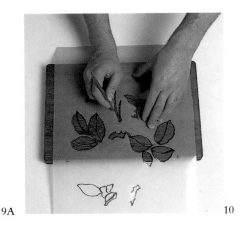

10

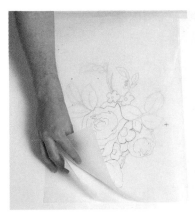

8

9B

11

7 Remove the Mylar, tape a third sheet over the pattern, and trace the registration marks and outlines of the large flowers.

8 You now have three sheets of Mylar, each with separate traced sections of the motif. Place them on top of each other with the registration marks aligned – you will see the complete pattern reformed.

Blocking-in and bridging:

9A Before cutting out the stencilled shapes you must draw in the position of the 'bridges'. These are thin strips introduced into the pattern in order to break it up into its component parts, thereby lending additional visual emphasis to each section, and giving support to the stencil sheet once it has been cut. Mark the bridges out with a felt-tip pen, positioned sympathetically; here, they emphasize the shapes of the leaves and flowers.

9B 'Blocking-in' is an extension of bridging; using a felt-tip pen, thicken up all the inner edges of the outlines.

Mark out bridges and block in on all three sheets of Mylar.

Cutting the stencil:

10 Place one of the traced sheets onto a cutting board. Hold the blade of a craft knife vertically over the pattern, and cut along the inner edges of the blocked-in outlines. Apply a continuous and steady pressure, and don't cut out the bridges.

11 When cutting around curves move the Mylar around the knife rather than the knife around the Mylar. This will ensure that the blade doesn't slip. When you have finished, cut out the other two sheets.

$\mathscr{S}$TENCIL PAINTING

Whether you buy pre-cut stencils or cut your own, whatever subjects you choose make sure they are in keeping with the style of the rest of the room – a simple basket of fruit will look very effective on a country kitchen pine door, but inappropriate on a lacquered coffee table in a modern dining room.

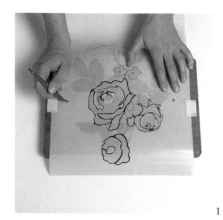

1

2

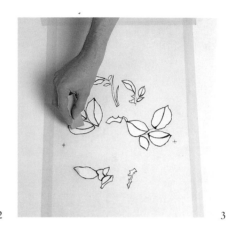

3

4

5

6

1 Secure the three sheets of Mylar on top of each other, using low-tack masking tape. With the registration marks on the sheets exactly aligned, make a small hole through them with the tip of a blade.

2 Using low-tack masking tape fix the leaf stencil into position on the surface to be decorated. With a pencil, lightly transfer the registration marks through the hole in the Mylar onto the surface.

3 Using a small piece of medium grade sandpaper, abrade the surface through the gaps in the Mylar, and remove any fine dust with a soft brush. This will key the finish for the stencil paint.

4 Mix up three slightly thinned matt or mid-sheen artists' acrylic glazes – red, green and lilac were used here. And test the colours on a piece of spare paper.

Acrylics are recommended for their fast drying times. This means you won't have to wait too long before you begin work with the second sheet of Mylar.

5 Dip a stencil brush into the green acrylic glaze, and remove any excess on a piece of spare paper – the brush should look almost dry. *Never* stencil with a brush clogged with paint – the final result will be unsuccessful.

Apply the paint through the stencil with a series of dabbing or pouncing movements, building up the colour slowly, in layers.

6 If you wish to introduce shading, or even an element of three-dimensionality, into the design, mix a little black with the green glaze, and gently add darker tones to sections of the leaves.

For the purposes of illustration I have shown you how to make a stencil from a sprig of flowers which were part of the pattern on a curtain. The technique includes an optional method of first tracing the design so that it can be enlarged or reduced in size on a photocopier, prior to cutting out the stencil (see page 134).

7

8

9

10

11

7 When you have finished stencilling the leaves, remove the low-tack masking tape and carefuly peel back the sheet of Mylar from the surface, without smudging the paint. If you intend to use the stencil again, wipe any paint from the surface of the Mylar, using a clean cloth.

8 When the green glaze has dried, tape the small flower stencil in position – very carefully lining up its registration marks over those applied to the surface through the leaf stencil.
Having lightly sanded the surface through the stencil and brushed away any dust, as in step 3, apply the lilac glaze using the same method as in steps 5 and 6. Then carefully peel back the sheet of Mylar as in step 7.

9 When the lilac glaze has dried, tape the large flower stencil in position. Again, carefully line up the registration marks with those on the surface; lightly sand through the stencil and brush away any dust, as in step 3, and apply the red glaze, as in steps 5 and 6.
10 Carefully peel back the sheet of Mylar to reveal the finished stencil. If you discover you have missed out any small sections of the glaze, these can be carefully touched in freehand with a small stencil brush.
11 Finally, when the paint has dried, apply one or two coats of matt or satin-finish clear polyurethane varnish for protection.

TORTOISESHELLING

Tortoiseshelling produces an elegant and striking finish on flat surfaces. However, on a large scale it can be rather overpowering, and is thus best confined to smaller items, such as side-table tops, picture or mirror frames (see page 117) and jewellery boxes.

Whilst it is a good idea to use a piece of real tortoiseshell for reference, don't be over-concerned with trying to

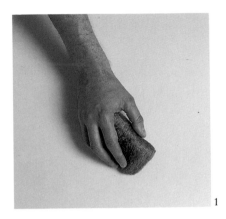

1 Having painted the surface to be decorated with an eggshell ground coat tinted with chrome or cadmium mid-yellow artists' oil (see page 123), cover it with a coat of matt or mid-sheen clear polyurethane varnish. And when the varnish has dried, rub it down with grade 00 wire wool.

2 Mix up a thin glaze consisting of 4 parts gloss finish clear polyurethane varnish, 2 parts white spirit and 1 part yellow ochre artists' oil (see page 123). Using a standard decorators' brush, apply the glaze evenly over the surface.

3 Whilst the glaze is still wet, dab it with a clean lint-free cloth to create a random mottled effect.

4 Mix up a glaze to the same proportions as in step 2, but this time substitute raw Sienna for the yellow ochre. Using a brush approximately half the size of the one used in step 2, apply the glaze in diagonal patches across the surface.

5 Spread and soften the patches created in the previous step, using a hog's hair softener. Then proceed to the next step before the glaze dries.

6 Darken the glaze used in step 4 with burnt umber artists' oil, and dab it onto the surface as smaller marks inside the patches created in step 4. Work in the same diagonal direction, and again proceed to the next stage before the glaze dries.

recreate an exact copy of it. Rather, concentrate on capturing the diagonal movement that is always present in the surface of the material.
Below I describe the method for producing a natural-looking yellow/brunette finish. However, substituting red and black colours, or tortoiseshelling over gilding (see pages 152–5), will produce equally dramatic alternatives.

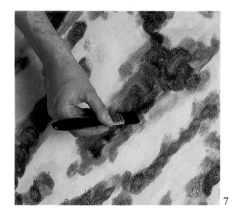

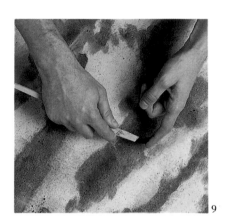

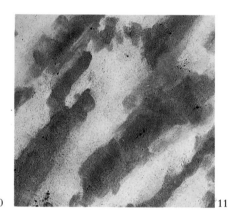

7 Add equal quantities of burnt umber and black to the glaze used in step 6. This will darken it further. Then, dab small blotches of it onto the centre of the patches created in step 6.

8 Before the glazes applied in steps 4–7 dry, soften and blend their edges together with a softening brush, and then repeat the process over the entire surface.

9 Using a small fitch or an old toothbrush, spatter (see page 132) a few droplets of the glaze used in step 7, mixed with some additional black, over the surface, to produce small, irregular-sized spots. Then, when they have nearly dried, gently soften them with the softening brush.

10 When the surface has dried, apply two coats of mid-sheen clear polyurethane varnish for protection. Gently rub down the final coat with fine grade 000 wire wool and then polish with wax and a soft cloth.

11 Buff regularly to improve the lustrous finish.

ℬAMBOOING

Bambooing, or faux bamboo, is a simple decorative technique for replicating the appearance of bamboo on any furniture that features rounded or turned legs and mouldings. There are two methods of bambooing. The first is picking out, which involves, as its name suggests, picking out in colour the knots or knobbly joints of real bamboo, and adding the decorative eyes and spines found on female bamboo. Obviously this technique is only applicable to the legs and framework of furniture that either is made of real bamboo or has been turned on a lathe to look like it.

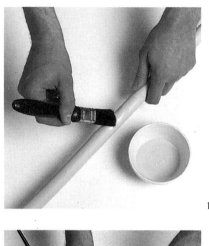

1

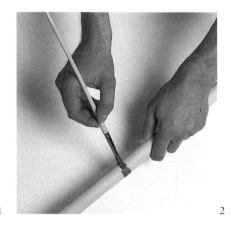

2

3

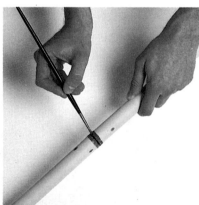

4

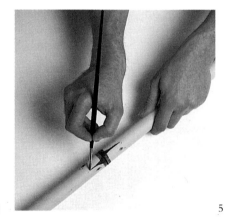

5

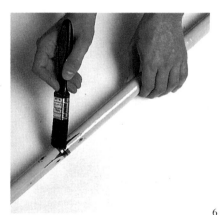

6

Picking out (natural finish)

1 Using a standard decorators' brush, apply one or two coats of flat-oil paint, coloured with yellow ochre artists' oil and a touch of burnt umber, to a previously prepared white flat-oil ground coat (see pages 118–21).

2 Mix up a little burnt umber artists' acrylic colour slightly thinned with water, so that it can be brushed on smoothly, and using a No 6 artists' brush paint a ring of pale colour around the centre of each knot or joint.

3 Using a No 3 artists' brush and the burnt umber, paint in the 'eyes'. They should be positioned on either side of the spines, but not evenly distributed between sections.

4 Darken the burnt umber acrylic with black, and again using a No 3 artists' brush, pick out the centre rings around the knuckles or joints.

5 Using the same coloured glaze and brush as in step 4, add the curved, spike-like spines above and below the knuckles. Then add a few fine specks of colour around the edges of the eyes (but don't overdo it), and carefully touch in their 'pupils' or centres.

6 When the paint has dried apply two coats of mid-sheen or gloss clear polyurethane varnish, both for protection and to give the finish either a soft sheen or a lacquered appearance.

The second method is bamboo striping, which can be applied to plain or unjointed legs and mouldings. Indeed the aim is to produce a pastiche of bamboo and suggest the presence of knots and joints by painting graduated rings in shades of the same colour on top of each other. There are no restrictions on the colours you can use. Obviously yellows and browns will look the most natural, but pastel pinks, blues and greens, and even black, will produce a very effective, if more flamboyant, finish.

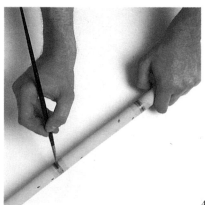

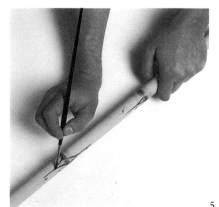

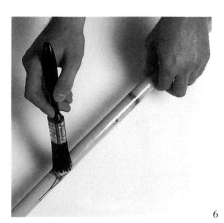

Bamboo striping (pastel finish)

1 Using a standard decorators' brush, apply one or two coats of a pastel coloured flat-oil paint to a previously prepared white flat-oil ground coat (see pages 118–21).
2 Make up a transparent coloured glaze by mixing artists' oil, in the colour of your choice, dissolved in 2 parts matt finish clear polyurethane varnish and a ½ part white spirit. There should only be a hint of colour in the glaze – and if striping over a dark ground add a touch of white to make it show up.
   Using a 2 cm (¾ in) standard decorators' brush, apply the glaze in

a series of rings about 2.5 cm (1 in) wide and at 15–20 cm (6–8 in) intervals along the leg or moulding. Allow to dry.
3 Darken the glaze made up in step 2 by adding more pigment and then, using a No 6 artists' brush, apply 1.2 cm (½ in) rings around the centre and on top of the rings applied in step 2. Then allow the glaze to dry.

4 Darken the glaze made up in step 3 by adding black and then, using a No 3 artists' brush, paint in the centre rings of the joints and dot in the eyes.
5 Using the same glaze and brush as in step 4, add the curved, spike-like spines above and below the joints. Then add a few fine specks of colour around the eyes and touch in their 'pupils' or centres.
6 When the glaze has dried apply two coats of mid-sheen or gloss clear polyurethane varnish, both for protection and to give the finish either a soft sheen or a lacquered appearance.

Wood-graining

Wood-graining is a traditional technique which enables you to reproduce faithful imitations of natural wood, or create fantasy wood finishes which display all manner of graining and colour.
Perhaps the most useful application of the technique is in the transformation of otherwise cheap, dull and boring pieces of furniture into seemingly valuable and elegant 'antiques'.
Consequently, the method I have outlined below is a simple way of simulating the grain of mahogany – a wood

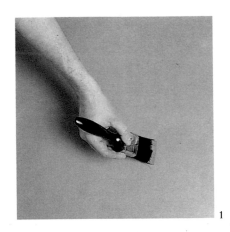

1 Having prepared the surface for decoration (see pages 118–20), apply two eggshell ground coats tinted with Indian red, burnt umber and a touch of black. The glaze should be a subdued but warm red colour (see page 122). Allow to dry.
2 Mix up a warm brown-coloured glaze of 4 parts scumble to 1 part white spirit, and tint it with 2 parts Van Dyck brown to 1 part burnt Sienna.
3 Using a standard decorators' brush, apply the glaze so that the brushmarks are roughly parallel, and in the direction that you want the grain to run.

4 To simulate mahogany heartwood: hold a standard decorators' brush as illustrated, and make a series (four or five) of elliptical and continuous sweeps through the glaze. The brushmarks should form shapes like very angular rugby balls – each one partially inside the previous one, and therefore of decreasing height and width.

5 Establish the side grain by dragging a standard decorators' brush in a series of straight sweeps on either side of the heart grain (it doesn't matter if you slightly overlap the edges of the heartwood). Slightly echo the curve of the outer elliptical shape, and occasionally make a very slight shimmering movement with your wrist, to ensure that the brushmarks aren't too straight.
6 Add a little black to the glaze mixed in step 2, and using a No 3 artists' brush touch in some darker lines on the inner apex of each elliptical heartwood shape, and on some of the side grain.

that is traditionally used in the manufacture of high-quality furniture.
To illustrate the various methods of replicating, for example, walnut, pine, maple and beech, is beyond the space
available here. However, the principles of mahogany graining can, with a little imagination, be adapted to
replicate the grains of other types of wood. And, by substituting different colours, fantasy wood finishes are easily
achieved. If you wish to try simulations of other woods, refer to a specialist book on the subject.

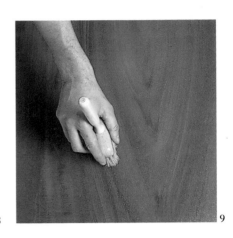

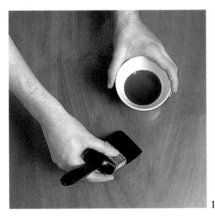

7 Whilst the glaze is still wet, use the tip of a hog's hair softener to lightly feather out and blend the grain of the heartwood. Work gradually towards the apex of the elliptical shapes, in a series of outwardly curving sweeps; that is, working against the curve of the heartwood. Don't press too hard, or you will obliterate the grain effect.

8 Now use the tip of the hog's hair softener to feather out and blend the side grain. Work in a series of short sweeps (it's a bit like using a feather duster) at 180 degrees to the direction of the grain. Again, don't press too hard.

9 Finally, use the tip of the hog's hair softener to stipple (see page 131) over any noticeable darker lines or patches of the glaze. This will create a fine, pore-like graining effect.

10 When the glaze has thoroughly dried, apply two coats of mid sheen or gloss clear polyurethane varnish, rubbing down with grade 00 wire wool between coats. If you wish to darken the appearance of the mahogany, add a little burnt umber to the varnish.

11 For an even more lustrous finish, when the varnish has dried apply a proprietary polish to the surface. Buff the polish to a deep shine with a clean, soft rag.

Lining

Lining is a decorative finish used to further embellish painted furniture. Coloured lines or stripes are applied by brush to the surface in order to accentuate the contours and features of the piece, and thereby emphasize its overall shape and proportions.

There are two different styles of lining – edge and fine. Edge lining involves painting broad bands of thinned coloured glaze around the edges of furniture, and is particularly appropriate for country style pieces such as kitchen tables and chests of drawers. And fine lining, as its name implies, is the application of thin lines of glaze towards

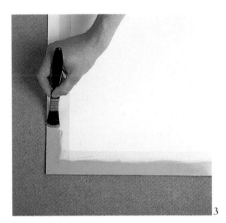

Edge lining

1 If you do not wish to edge line freehand (which is quite difficult, even on very small objects), mark out the previously prepared surface (see pages 118–21) with low-tack masking tape. Hexagonal corners can be coped with by cutting the tape with a craft knife. Depending on the size of the piece of furniture, the edge line should be 1–3 cm (½–1½ ins) wide.

2 Mix up a slightly thinned glaze in the colour of your choice, using artists' oils or acrylics (see pages 122–3) – a drop of liquid detergent added to an acrylic glaze will help it stick to the surface.

3 Using a 1.2 cm (½ in) standard decorators' brush, apply the glaze to the masked-off edges. When the glaze has dried you may wish to apply a further coat(s) to build up the depth of colour.

If you don't intend to use masking tape: use a specialist lining brush or a fitch, employ a steady sweeping movement, don't hold the brush too tightly or too near the bristles and

practice on spare paper first – though any mistakes can be immediately rubbed out with a rag dipped in white spirit or water.

4 Carefully remove the masking tape.

5 If any glaze has crept under the edge and has dried, (or if your freehand line is a bit wobbly), very carefully and gently scrape it off with a craft knife.

And finally, if you wish to produce a faded antique finish, rub the dried glaze with grade 00 wire wool, prior to applying two coats of matt or mid-sheen clear polyurethane varnish for protection.

the centre of a piece in order to highlight features, strengthen shape and define separate sections of colour and pattern. It is a finish more suited to fine, elegant furniture and small items such as trays, picture frames and boxes, than larger and cruder items.
Of course, edge and fine lining can be successfully combined, as in our illustrations below. But whichever style or combination you use, it will usually look most effective when applied over the top of another elegant paint finish, such as dragging (see page 128), lacquering (see page 146), or colourwashing (see page 133).

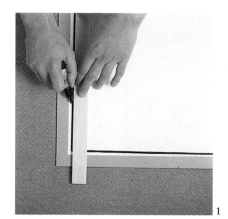

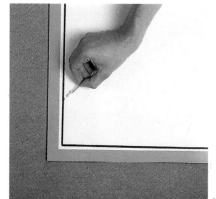

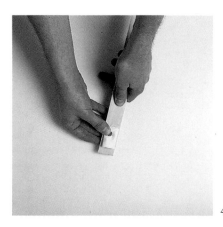

Fine lining

1 The simplest method of fine lining is to use a straight edge and an indelible ink felt-tip pen. Thus, position a rule at the required distance from, and parallel to, the edge. And mark out the fine lines with the pen — waiting for each line to dry (this will be almost immediately) before re-positioning the ruler for the next one.
2 If ink has crept under the straight edge, remove it from the surface with a cotton wool bud moistened in white spirit.

3 A more traditional method is to mix up a slightly thinned glaze in the colour of your choice, using artists' oils or acrylics (see pages 122–3) — a drop of liquid detergent added to an acrylic glaze will help it stick to the surface. Then, having first practised on a spare piece of paper, position the straight edge, charge a No 3 artists' sable brush with glaze, removing any excess and, with the lower part of the handle pressed at a slight angle against the rule, pull the brush along the line in a continuous movement. Adopt a relaxed but steady approach, and wipe out any mistakes straight away with a

cotton wool bud dipped in white spirit or water.
4 When you have finished the first line, pin two small rolls of material to the back ends of the straight edge, so that it can be positioned for the next line by bridging the first one, and thereby avoid smudging the still wet glaze.
5 Finally, if you wish to produce a faded antique finish, rub the dried glaze with grade 00 wire wool, prior to applying two coats of matt or mid-sheen clear polyurethane varnish for protection.

LACQUERING

techniques

The technique of lacquering (or japanning) outlined below will provide the surface of any suitable piece of furniture with a smooth, shiny and lustrous finish. Whilst being only a pastiche of an original Oriental lacquered finish, which involved the laborious application of up to 40 layers of glaze, this method is a quick, convincing and elegant alternative. However, to achieve the best results some time must be spent on preparation of the surface, as the required smooth finish is dependent on an equally smooth ground coat.

Lacquering is most suited to plain furniture, such as coffee tables, cabinets and chests, and smaller items like jewellery boxes. Fussy pieces adorned with features and mouldings are not as appropriate. But whatever the item,

1

2

3

4

1 Using a standard decorators' brush, apply three coats of black flat-oil paint, thinned with a little white spirit, to a previously prepared ground coat. The underlying surface should have been thoroughly prepared to a smooth finish (see pages 118–21); any grain or imperfections having been filled with three or four coats of a thin solution of fine grade surface filler – each coat being rubbed down with fine-grade sandpaper, prior to priming and undercoating.

2 When the final coat of black flat-oil has dried, rub it down with fine grade wet-and-dry paper and soapy water, and allow to dry.
3 Mix up a glaze or lacquer consisting of 5 parts black flat-oil paint, 1 part burnt umber (artists' oil) and a ½ part gloss finish clear polyurethane varnish.
4 Using a standard decorators' brush, apply two coats of glaze to the surface, rubbing down with fine grade wet-and-dry paper and soapy water after both coats. Allow to dry.

it need not be made of high quality materials: plywood or melamine-faced chipboard, provided it has been prepared properly (see below), will provide just as good a surface as oak or pine, for example.
Traditionally, the majority of lacquered pieces were either a deep black or red (vermilion) colour. However, other colours such as white, green, yellow and blue were and can be used with spectacular results.
Finally, whilst a plain-coloured, unadorned lacquer finish will look very chic in a modern setting, if you wish to enhance the oriental effect for a more traditional look, you can hand paint or stencil (see pages 134–7) appropriate Eastern motifs on top of the layers of paint prior to varnishing.

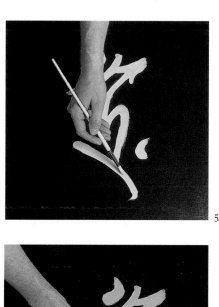
5

6

7

8

5 Apply any handpainted or stencilled motifs at this stage (see pages 134–7). In this example, a No 6 artists' brush and a slightly thinned yellow glaze was used to paint freehand an adaptation of a Japanese character.
6 When the glaze has dried, apply a minimum of three coats of gloss finish polyurethane varnish, tinted with a little burnt umber artists' oil and thinned in a ratio of 3 parts varnish to 2 parts white spirit. Adding the burnt umber, which is optional, will give warmth to the finish.
7 Rub down each coat with fine grade 000 wire wool and soapy water, and allow to dry thoroughly before applying the next coat.
8 When the final coat of varnish is dry, it should be polished with a beeswax or silicone polish and a clean soft rag in order to obtain a deep, lustrous finish.

ᴀntiquing

Antiquing is a method of simulating the effects of age on furniture. As such it is a useful device for restoring authenticity to items which have been recently repaired or renovated and, as a result, now look too pristine or new. Equally, it is a way of adding character to, and softening the appearance of, modern pieces which are rather stark and featureless, and of suggesting quality and craftsmanship in cheap and functional 'junk' store items.

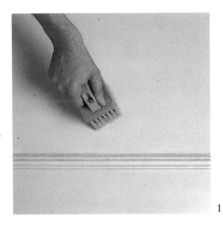

1

2

3

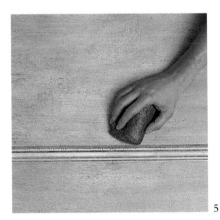

4

5

1 To a previously prepared flat-oil or eggshell ground (see pages 118–21), apply a matt or eggshell finish in the colour of your choice. Here a jade green glaze has been stippled on (see page 131).
2 When the glaze has dried, apply a coat of matt or mid-sheen clear polyurethane varnish. This will enable you to remove any mistakes made whilst antiquing, without causing any damage to the underlying paint finish.

3 Mix up a thin transparent glaze of artists' oil colour and white spirit (see pages 122–3), and add a dash of white flat oil paint to give just a touch of opacity. Use dull earth colours such as jade green darkened with a burnt umber or burnt Sienna and a touch of black. By using the underlying ground colour (in this case, jade green) as a main constituent of the glaze, you will reduce the risk of too strong a contrast with the paint finish below.
4 Using a standard decorators' brush, apply a thin coat of the glaze to the surface of the piece of furniture.

5 Whilst the glaze is still tacky, gently rub down the entire surface with grade 00 wire wool. This will lift off some of the glaze and reveal the underlying ground colour, thus creating gently graduated areas of light and shade. For authenticity, press harder on raised mouldings and the tops of chair arms and tables; that is, those areas where you would expect the greatest amount of wear and tear.

The object of the technique is to mimic or replicate certain specific aspects of ageing: the build-up of a deep, lustrous patina; the accumulation of dust and dirt which results in shading over the surface; the wearing away and cracking of paint and varnish, and the softening and toning down of colours. On certain items, such as desks, it can even involve the deliberate application of faded ink stains!

6

7

8

 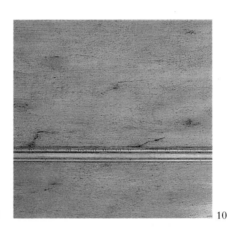

9

10

6 An optional, but authentic-looking touch is to mix up a darker glaze, or use permanent ink, and spatter a few tiny droplets over the surface (see page 132). This will simulate the random spots of contrasting colour associated with the painted surface of antique pieces. You shouldn't overdo it though.

7 Now dip a No 3 artists' brush in the darker glaze or ink, and lightly feather in some broken streaks over the surface, especially close to any mouldings. This will simulate the random splits and cracks that appear in the painted surfaces of antique furniture.

8 When the 'spots' and 'cracks' have dried (or are still just tacky), tone them down by gently rubbing with fine grade 000 wire wool.

9 When the glaze has thoroughly dried, apply two coats of matt or mid-sheen clear polyurethane varnish. If you wish to further darken the antique finish, add a little burnt umber or black artists' oil to the varnish. (For authenticity, you can even sprinkle a small quantity of dust into the crevices of the mouldings, after applying the second coat – it will be permanently stuck in position by the varnish.)

10 When the second coat of varnish has dried, lightly rub it down with fine grade 000 wire wool, and finish off by polishing the surface with beeswax or silicone polish and a soft cloth. Polish regularly to establish a deep and lustrous patina.

$\mathcal{M}$ARBLING

The technique of marbling involves either reproducing an accurate copy of a specific marble, or creating a fantasy finish that to all intents and purposes looks like marble, without actually being any particular type. In either case, the mere suggestion of marble will lend an air of opulence to almost any piece of furniture.
The many different types of marble have a number of qualities in common, and it is these that you must try to capture successfully in paint. Irregular veining systems, translucency of colour, and a sense of monumentality, density and weight are the most important characteristics.
The technique outlined below is a way of reproducing White Vein marble – perhaps the best-known variety.

1

2

3

4

5

1 Mix up three separate coloured glazes by adding raw umber and yellow ochre to Payne's gray (see page 123). Make each glaze a different tone of gray by varying the proportions of the three colours. But make sure they are very thin and transparent – they are intended only to discolour the ground coat.
2 Using a clean rag, wipe a thin coat of scumble glaze, slightly thinned with white spirit, over the surface of a previously prepared smooth, white eggshell ground (see pages 118–21).

3 Using a separate small standard decorators' brush for each of the glazes, apply them over the wet scumble ground in a series of uneven, irregular and broken channels. Employ a stippling and dabbing action and work diagonally across the surface.

4 Work over the entire surface, but don't overlap the three glazes and leave quite a bit of the white ground coat exposed. Those areas or channels where the darkest of the glazes is applied will determine the path of the veins, and thus the appearance of the finished marble – so make sure you either follow this illustration, or refer to a real piece of White Vein throughout.
5 Whilst the glazes are still wet, pull a dry hog's hair softening brush over the surface to soften the glazes and blend their edges together. Work in all directions, but concentrate on the diagonal movement used in step 3.

White Vein is a translucent stone that features an irregular gray veining system, displaying blue, green and yellow discolourations against a white mottled ground. It is often used for fire surrounds and table tops, though it can be applied to almost any piece of furniture, provided the basic pattern is not overstated.
Once you have marbled White Vein, for a fantasy finish repeat the technique but substitute different colours when scumbling and veining the white ground. Beyond that, look at other interior design books, or visit museums, featuring different types of marble. You will find that Sienna, Yellow onyx, Breccia, Bois Jourdan and the many varieties of Serpentine are all elegant and colourful finishes for furniture.

6

7

8

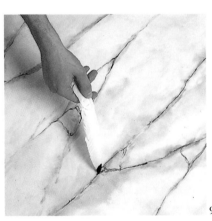
9

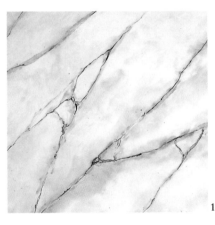
10

6 Mix up a mid-gray transparent glaze by blending Payne's gray and raw umber artists' oils with white spirit and a small quantity of scumble (see page 123). Charge a No 6 artists' brush with the glaze, and apply the secondary veins using a fidgety dithering action. The veins follow roughly diagonal paths and tend to accentuate the darker channels in the ground below.

7 Immediately the secondary veins have been applied they must be softened with the hog's hair brush, in order to make them appear to lie below the surface. Pull the brush both along their diagonal lengths, and at right angles — sometimes reducing the pressure so that some of the veins will appear nearer the surface. Then allow the softened surface to dry.
8 Using a brush or rag, apply a thin coat of scumble glaze, thinned with a little white spirit, over the secondary veins.

9 Make up a slightly darker and more opaque version of the glaze used in step 6 by adding a little black and using less white spirit. Then, using a goose feather (a No 3 artists' brush is an acceptable substitute), apply the glaze to establish the primary veins. Follow the illustration to establish their position, and gently soften all but the finest ones with the hog's hair brush.
10 When the surface has dried, apply two coats of mid-sheen clear polyurethane varnish, both for protection and to add a lustrous (rather than glossy) quality to the finish.

GOLD AND METAL LEAF GILDING

Gilding with gold leaf is a traditional and very effective way of embellishing furniture and artefacts. Gold leaf and its cheaper metal alloy substitutes are available from artists' suppliers as booklets containing sheets of the gold or alloy supported on wax tissue. Some of the alloys look like gold and others can be tinted with orange shellac to simulate it. All of them can be gently rubbed down in places with fine grade 000 wire wool to reveal a hint of the underlying ground colour and thus simulate the wear and tear of ageing. Similarly, the application of tinted

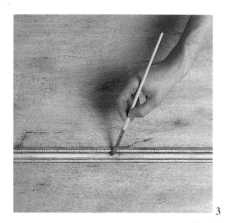

1 For the purposes of illustration gold leaf is shown being applied to a section of a previously antiqued surface (see page 148). Consequently, those areas to be gilded must first be rubbed down with 0 grade wire wool to key the varnish.

2 Remove any grease, dust and debris by cleaning the surface with a clean lint-free rag and white spirit.

3 Using a No 6 artists' brush, apply a coat of goldsize (available from artists' suppliers) to the moulding.

4 Again using a No 6 artists' brush, apply a coat of goldsize to the section below the moulding. It is a good idea to add a touch of colour (artists' oil) to the goldsize, so that it shows up against the background. Here, a pelmet-shaped border has been applied freehand under the moulding. But you can try any pattern or motif, and use a stencil to help with the outline (see pages 134–7).

5 When the goldsize is tacky (it should take a fingerprint), place a sheet of gold leaf on top of a section of the moulding. Using an artists' brush (very effective for crevices) or cotton wool, rub over the wax paper backing, applying a firm and even pressure all over. Then carefully lift off the wax paper to leave the gold leaf stuck in position.

Continue this process with as many leaves as are necessary to cover the required surface area. Each strip of leaf should slightly overlap the previous one, but don't worry if you are unable to fill every bump and crevice – it will contribute to the antique effect.

varnishes will create a convincing antique effect.
The leaf is very versatile and can be applied to carvings and mouldings as well as flat surfaces. But it is perhaps
most effective when enhancing selected highlights of a piece, such as drawer fronts, desk tops or chair legs, or
smaller items such as jewellery boxes or picture frames. A rule of thumb with gilding is: never overdo it; given its
striking appearance, a little gold leaf goes a long way.

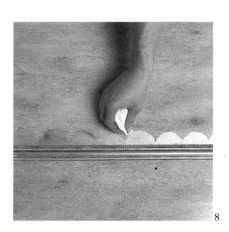

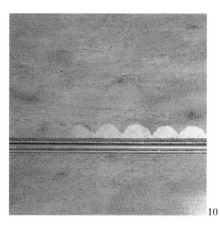

6 Now repeat the gilding process as above, gradually working your way along the pelmet motif. As the surface is flat, you will only need to use cotton wool to rub the back of the wax paper and transfer the gold leaf.

7 Using an artists' brush (or a hog's hair softener), carefully sweep off any metal debris from the surface. If you accidentally scrape or tear the gold leaf, simply repair it by rubbing on another small patch. You will have about three or four hours before the goldsize dries.

8 If you need to tidy up the edges of the pelmet motif, moisten a strip of clean rag with white spirit, wrap it around your finger and carefully rub off the excess gold leaf.

9 When the goldsize has dried (three or four hours), either rub over it with cotton wool to smooth out any ridges and bumps, or gently rub it down with fine grade 000 wire wool for a faded, worn antique effect (optional). Then brush on a coat of mid-sheen clear polyurethane varnish thinned with white spirit (see pages 122–3) and tinted with raw or burnt umber artists' oil. This will add to the antique effect. If you have used metal leaf, apply two coats of orange shellac to turn it into

'gold'. (Or apply watered-down Indian ink to aluminium leaf, to produce 'silver'.)

10 When the entire surface has dried, apply two coats of mid-sheen clear polyurethane varnish, rubbing down with fine grade 000 wire wool before and after the second coat. Then wax and polish with a soft rag.

GILDING WITH METAL POWDERS

Metallic powders provide a cheaper alternative to gilding with gold leaf – as you will discover, a little powder goes a long way. They are readily available from artists' suppliers and, if applied as thin strips or delicate motifs, rather than as large, flat expanses – which look overpowering – they provide a very successful gold or silver gilded embellishment to pieces of furniture, and small artefacts such as jewellery boxes.

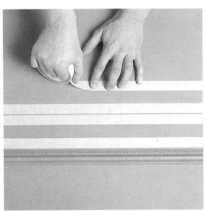

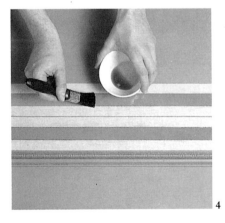

1 To a previously prepared surface that has been primed and undercoated (see pages 118–21), apply two coats of a slightly thinned eggshell glaze in the colour of your choice. The glaze should complement or contrast with the metal powder – in this case, silver.
2 Using a pencil and ruler, draw the faint outlines of the area to be gilded. In this case the intention is to gild two parallel lines below a section of moulding – the sort of pattern you might care to try around the perimeter of a chest or trunk.
3 Run lengths of low-tack masking tape along the pencil outlines to mask off the two parallel strips.

4 Using a small standard decorators' brush, apply a coat of clear polyurethane varnish to the surface, between the strips of masking tape. Make sure you don't miss out any patches, or the powder will come away at a later stage.

5 When the varnish becomes tacky, pour some silver metal powder into the lid of the powder jar, and wrap an offcut of chamois leather smoothly round your finger. Dip your chamois-covered finger into the powder, and as you will need only a small amount, brush off any excess back into the jar. Then, position your finger on the surface within the masking tape and make gentle rotating and circling movements to distribute and polish the powder. Pick up more powder from the plate as you need to. (If you are applying or mixing different coloured powders on the surface, you must use a new piece of chamois leather for each one).

The appearance of the metal powders can be enhanced considerably by applying them on top of contrasting or complementary colours, such as red or black or yellow, or wood-grained finishes, and then coating them with tinted varnishes or Indian ink to create a faded antique effect. Moreover, the method of applying the powders lends itself to motifs that use stencil (see pages 134–7) or masking tape (see below) outlines.

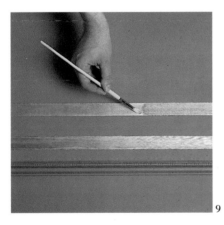

6 When you have finished applying the powder, carefully peel back the masking tape.

7 It is very important to leave the surface for a minimum of 36 hours whilst the underlying varnish dries out. Failure to do so may result in the powder spreading or coming off altogether during the next stage.

8 When the varnish has dried, use a clean rag wrapped around your finger and some soapy water (liquid detergent will do) to gently rub down the powder gilding. You will find that quite a lot of loose powder will come off onto the rag. If you rub harder you may find some of the underlying ground colour beginning to ghost through. This will be very effective – but only if you are trying to create a slightly worn antiqued finish.

9 Again for an antique finish, use either thinned Indian ink, or a glaze made up of 2 parts mid-sheen clear polyurethane varnish to 1 part white spirit, tinted with a little dark blue artists' oil, and apply it to the silver powder gilding with a No 6 artists'

brush. Take care not to brush the glaze onto the surrounding surface. You may need to apply a second coat depending on how 'old' or dark you want the silver to look.

10 When the ink or glaze has dried, apply two coats of mid-sheen or gloss polyurethane varnish to the entire surface for protection.

$\mathscr{T}$ROMPE L'OEIL

Trompe l'oeil means 'to deceive the eye'. It is a traditional technique of decorative paintwork which is intended to fool the onlooker, even if only momentarily, into believing that he or she is looking at a three-dimensional object or scene, such as a vase or picture frame, or even a panoramic view of the countryside, rather than a two-dimensional flat-painted picture.

Because the deception is created by using light, shade and perspective, a degree of artistic ability is required. However, by initially restricting yourself to geometric shapes, such as mock panelling on a cupboard door (as below), you will achieve successful results quite quickly. Indeed, the application of such a trompe l'oeil *on a run*

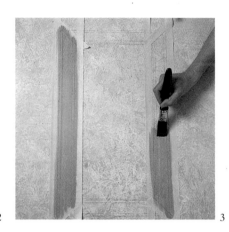

1 Onto a previously ragged finish (see page 130), copy the outlines of the frame, using a ruler and a soft lead pencil.

2 Mask off two opposite sides of the frame, including the mitred corners.

3 Mix up two batches of a thick glaze (see page 123) in a ratio of 70 percent scumble, 10 percent white spirit and 20 percent eggshell in the colour used for the ragged background. Apply the glaze within the masked-off areas, using a standard decorators' brush. Before it dries, remove the tape and clean up any uneven edges (see step 4, below). Note: the pencil lines should

ghost faintly through the glaze.

4 When the glaze has dried, repeat steps 2 and 3 for the top and bottom of the frame. Clean wet ragged edges by running a folded rag moistened in white spirit along them.

5 To introduce an element of 'three-dimensionality', apply bands of glaze to represent softly diffused light reflecting off the curved surfaces of the frame. Carefully copy the illustration to determine their different widths and positions, noting that the predominant light source is off-left. Mask off the bands one at a time (remember the

mitred corners) with low-tack tape, using the pencil guidelines to help you where appropriate, before applying a paler version of the glaze used in step 3 (just add white eggshell to it).

6 When masking off the bands, note that where the bands meet at the top right and bottom left-hand corners they are staggered; whereas on the opposite diagonal they meet evenly.

of old melamine kitchen units can dramatically transform them into a seemingly 'hand-built', 'one-off' kitchen – especially when applied over another finish, such as ragging.
In the example below, the lines of perspective and the subsequent application of subtle shades of colour are determined by a predominant light source that is off-left, at approximately 10.00 hrs. By copying these illustrations you will learn a great deal about perspective and the way light casts shadows over a moulded surface. Hopefully, this will give you the confidence to then choose both your own subjects for trompe l'oeil, *and to vary the position of the predominant light source.*

7

8

9

10

11

7 Strengthen the appearance of 'three-dimensionality' by applying thin bands of glaze to represent the predominant light source reflecting off the edges and apex of the curved surfaces of the frame. Again, carefully copy the illustration to determine the position of these 'highlights'. Mask them off one at a time (remember the mitred corners), and apply a white eggshell glaze (tinted with a little of the glaze used in step 5), using a No 3 artists' brush.

8 Mask off the areas of shadow cast by the frame onto the background. Carefully copy the illustration to

determine their position and width, noting that they are cast away from the light source, and that they underpin the appearance of 'three-dimensionality'. Colour in with a stencil brush and a thin film of the glaze used in step 3 – sweep, rather than dab it on.

9 If you are creating a *trompe l'oeil* cupboard door, use a soft lead pencil to draw the outline of the door knob slightly offset against its backplate, and add the elongated shadow it casts, as in the illustration. Then, with a No 3 artists' brush, colour in the knob with the white glaze used in step 7, and the backplate with the

pale glaze used in step 5.

10 Colour in the shadow with the artists' brush and the darker glaze used in step 3, and carefully dab and pounce the wet glaze with the stencil brush, to soften it. And pounce the now-dirty brush over the knob to create a little shading on its surface.

11 When the glaze has dried, apply two coats of matt or mid-sheen clear polyurethane varnish for protection.

INDEX

$\mathscr{A}$CKNOWLEDGEMENTS

The publishers would like to thank the following for their kind permission to reproduce the photographs in this book:

Richard Bryant/Arcaid 31, 36, 60–1, 79, 93; Lucinda Lambton/Arcaid 68, 107; Bridgeman Art Library 9, 11, 12, 14T, 15; The Royal Pavilion, Art Gallery and Museums of Brighton 10B; Michael Boys 17, 37B, 58B, 59, 75T, 77B, 100, 108, 115; Camera Press 20, 38L, 38R, 56R, 76, 112R; The Charleston Trust 30T; Christie's Colour Library 10T, 14B; Dragons of Walton Street 84, 85, 86, 87, 92TL, 92BL, 94B; Elizabeth Whiting Associates 43, 54, 75B, 77T; The Futon Company 23; National Magazine Co. Ltd – Photographer: Arabella Ashley/Courtesy of Country Living 24, 24–5, 102, 103, 104, 104–5; The National Trust Photographic Library 8, 13; The National Trust for Scotland 16; Sanderson 67; Smallbone of Devizes 52, 55, 78, 80; Syndication International – Homes and Gardens 32, 53, 66, 69, 113; World of Interiors/Bill Batten 63; World of Interiors/John Mason 74; World of Interiors/James Mortimer 109T.

All commissioned photography by Jon Bouchier.

Paint techniques by Paul Rackham, *trompe l'oeil* by Sally Kenny.

The publishers would also like to thank the following manufacturers for supplying materials for photography: C. Brewer and Sons (of Putney); Frank Romany Ltd.; London Graphics Centre.

Also special thanks to Nessa Kearney, Nessa Quinn, Penny Rogers and the Dragons Studio, and to Mrs Patti Bryant of Henfield and Mrs Govier of Sevenoaks for allowing us to photograph their homes.

Every effort has been made to trace the copyright holders and we apologise in advance for any unintentional omissions and would be pleased to insert the appropriate acknowledgements in any subsequent edition of this publication.

My warmest thanks to all who helped so much with this book. Firstly to Judith More, my Editor, whose great idea it was! To Jane Laing who did so much so well, and without whose help I would have been lost. To Dragons Studio artists, especially Nessa Kearney. Very many thanks too to artists Hannerley Dehn, Jane Maiden, Nessa Quinn, Tony Raymond, John Osborne, Colleen and Robert Bery, Sue Jackson, Stephen Hesmondhalgh and Andree Langhorn. Finally, I would like to thank Mrs Govier and Mrs Bryant for their kind permission in allowing us to use their homes.

Rosie Fisher